Regional Administr[a]
in Japan

In Japan, the main local administrative affairs are traditionally allotted to prefectures and municipalities, while communal disposal systems, firefighting, and regional development take secondary importance. However, two new changes to the frame of local governments have altered the main frameworks of national and provincial governance. With decentralization reforms taking effect, more local bodies are gaining autonomy and departing from uniformity. This has allowed methods of cooperation between governing bodies to diversify – trends which augur a dissolution of uniformity in Japanese local administration. If left alone, it may eventually lead to disparities between principal and peripheral bodies, and thus complicate the administrative systems further. How will these changes affect future community development? This book aims to address the dynamism of concepts of wide-area public service in Japan. It advocates the use of flexible strategies to ensure service standards are best suited to each regional demand. This concept can be called "departure from uniformity." This book also examines the advantages and disadvantages of these shifts for the future of Japanese public policy, and suggests various strategies to prevent further complications (e.g., autonomous settlement zones).

Regional Administration in Japan will interest researchers of Japanese public policy and public administration. This book will also engage researchers of Japanese politics and Japanese studies in general.

Shunsuke Kimura is Professor at the Graduate School of Law in Hitotsubashi University, Japan.

Routledge Contemporary Japan Series

For a full list of titles in this series, please visit www.routledge.com

Regional Administration in Japan
Departure from uniformity

Shunsuke Kimura

LONDON AND NEW YORK

First published 2017
by Routledge

2 Park Square, Milton Park, Abingdon, Oxfordshire OX14 4RN
711 Third Avenue, New York, NY 10017

Routledge is an imprint of the Taylor & Francis Group, an informa business

First issued in paperback 2017

British Library Cataloguing in Publication Data
A catalogue record for this book is available from the British Library

Library of Congress Cataloging-in-Publication Data
A catalog record for this book has been requested

ISBN: 978-1-138-64025-2 (hbk)
ISBN: 978-0-8153-6152-7 (pbk)

Typeset in Times New Roman
by Apex CoVantage, LLC

Contents

Figures

viii *Figures*

Tables

1 Introduction: "departure from the uniformity"

Japanese experience of regional administration

Introduction

In the local administrative system, the structure of local governments is essential. Japan has two types of local governments: ordinary local governments (ordinary governments) and special local governments (special governments). The ordinary governments are prefectures and municipalities. The special governments are unions and similar entities. Unions comprise partial-affairs associations (PAA) and regional unions, which have mostly controlled a variety of regional public services, such as garbage disposal, firefighting, and regional-level development. Regional unions have played an important part in the regional administrative approaches manifest in a variety of forms, such as unions, councils, shared administrative organizations, delegation of duties, and dispatch of personnel.

In Japan, ordinary governments have principal roles in the local administrations, and special governments fulfill supplementary yet crucial functions. However, ordinary governments have recently undergone significant changes. Generally, national laws determine their functions; however, these functions have been enlarged by decentralization reforms. Simultaneously, the number of ordinary governments has markedly decreased because of the major amalgamation movement that occurred between 1999 and 2010, in which the number of municipalities decreased from 3,229 to 1,771. These substantial changes significantly influenced the structure of special governments. Moreover, local administrations have been influenced by numerous social changes and agendas, such as rapidly decreasing populations, low birth rates, and an aging population, which shrinks the proportions of taxpayers, widens regional differences, slows decentralization, and so on. Under these conditions, broad public services have been significantly challenged.

The goal of this book is to review the dynamism of the concepts relevant to Japan's regional administrative system in this context. It addresses three basic questions:

1 What are the characteristics of the Japanese system?
2 What are the recent changes?
3 What new agenda confronts the Japanese local administration system?

Traditionally, the basic concept of the Japanese local administration is to establish the national minimum and improve the regional standards of service in which residents should be provided the same level of public services across regions. However, those ideas are beginning to change.

There are two new thematic trends. First, it is expected that proactive separate transitions will continue changing into an effective cooperative style, and rapid transition to this suitable style is anticipated in local administrations. One of the challenges of the traditional wide-area administrative methods such as PAA is that it is difficult to obtain a speedy consensus among the affiliated local governments. Responding to those issues, the Local Autonomy Law (LAL) introduced a simple process by which an affiliate could secede from an association (PAA or council) for the transition to more suitable types.

Second, a new type of wide-area administrative method was introduced: the autonomous settlement zone (ASZ) system.

The declining birthrate and growing proportion of elderly people, the dramatic depopulation, and the tight state finances began in Japan at the beginning of the 21st century. Under these conditions, the idea that all the municipalities should take on the full set of public service functions fell into difficulty, and the idea changed from raising the level of the total unit to approving the spillover functions of the central city in the region. This idea is based on the today's status of the regional situation, in which the region's central city is responsible for spillover functions by providing some services, such as medical, social welfare, and transportation, to the peripheral areas.

In this perspective, the local jurisdictions support each other by using the principal cities' spillover function. This demonstrates a change from the unitary national minimum that indicates a concept of a farewell to the bottom up as the regional development strategy.

Moreover, the ASZ system has the following two characteristics:

1 Shifting from the joint agreement to one-to-one agreement: the traditional and typical wide-area administrative method is PAA. PAA is established based on the joint legal act by several local governments. On the other hand, the ASZ is based on the contract between one central

city to each of the other neighbor municipalities. This is called one-to-one agreement, which is easier to amend based on the negotiation between the two local governments. This type of method leads the more flexible inter-municipal relationship in the current regions.

2 The style of regional development measure shifts from setting organization to formulating the substantial agreements among the local governments.

Under the policy of setting up the regional administrative zone (RAZ, stated in Chapter 4), establishing the organizations as administrators is a crucial process. On the other hand, under the policy of ASZ the contents of one-to-one agreement are thought to be significant. This is a change in the regional development policy and the ASZ method is thought to be reasonable and effective.

In this manner the wide-area administrative methods and the regional development policies are dramatically changing in the current local administration.

When reviewing these themes, it is important to consider the background of Japan's local administrative system. Therefore, Chapter 2 describes the basic structure of Japan's local government and Chapter 3 explains the basic structure of the current regional administrative system. Then, Chapter 4 covers the recent changes to the administrative structure and Chapter 5 offers conclusions concerning the future of the regional administration.

It is my hope that this book furthers our understanding of this phase of Japan's local administration.

2 The basic structure of Japan's local government

History of local autonomy in Japan

The advancement of Japan's system of local governance has proceeded along the same path of change as the structure of its local public entities. An overview of the history is presented in this chapter.

The pioneer period

Before 1860, Japanese governance was characterized by the feudal system, a ruling *shogun* (a hereditary commander-in-chief) who dominated the lords, and *hanshu* (the domain lords) who collected rents from the villages. In this structure, the *han* (clan) was the administrative unit and the villages were not administrative units; they were factual entities.

The Meiji Restoration was the restoration of imperial power in 1867, and it was the starting point of Japan as a nation-state. The standing of the *hans* and villages dramatically changed because the national government replaced feudal governance with a modern local administrative system, based on *hans* and territorial boundaries of prefectures, before the promulgation of the Imperial Constitution. In this way, the factual entities began to transition into modern local governments.

In 1878, *San-shin-pou* (Three New Ordinances) marked the first step in the history of modern local governance. The Municipal Formation Ordinance divided prefectures into *gun* (counties) and *ku* (cities), and then subdivided counties into *cho* and *son* (towns and villages, respectively). Three of these levels, *ku, cho,* and *son*, had dual identities as local governments and national administrative constituencies. The Prefectural Assembly Ordinance introduced prefectural assemblies composed of elected members, and the Local Tax Ordinance provided procedures for collecting local taxes and identified prefectures as local authorities to some extent. Table 2.1 provides the chronology of the evolution of the Japanese local administrative system.

Table 2.1 Chronology of the Japanese system of local government

Chronology

1878	Three new laws (*San-Shin-Pou*: the counties, towns and villages organization law, etc.)	First-time local administration legal systems
1888–1889	The Great Meiji Consolidation	The number of municipalities decreased from 71,314 to 15,859
1888	Start of implementation of the City Law and the Town and Village Law	Main act of basic local public entities
1891	Start of implementation of the Prefectural Law and the County Law	Main act of local public entities of upper tier
1943	Implementation of the Tokyo Metropolitan system	
1947	Implementation of the Constitution of Japan	The formulation of the democratic administrative systems were advanced
1947	Implementation of the Local Autonomy Law	Main postwar act of local public entities
1953–1956	The Great Showa Consolidation	The number of municipalities decreased from 9,868 to 3,975
1999	The Great Heisei Consolidation	The number of municipalities decreased from 3,229 to 1,771
2000	Implementation of the Uniform Decentralization Law	The transfer of administrative powers and responsibilities put seriously on the move
2008	The framework of the autonomous settlement zones (ASZ) started.	This framework correspond in position to the post–Great Heisei Consolidation
2014	The framework of the cooperated nerve city zone started.	This framework deals with the population diminishment through the local revitalization.

Source: Created by the author.

The pre–World War II period of development under the Imperial Constitution

In 1881, an Imperial Ordinance created the National Diet to commence in 1890. The government attempted at that time to install full-fledged local governance to be implemented before the National Diet to familiarize the public with aspects of modern democracy. Thus, in 1889, the Shisei (city act)

and the Chosonsei (town/village act) were implemented, which was the first time that an overall legal system was installed at the local level. The Municipal Government Act was modeled primarily on the Prussian local administrative system, although it accounted for the unique features of traditional Japanese society. The Municipal Government Act provided for municipal assemblies of elected members to serve as the legislative administrators of the municipalities. Mayors of *cho* (town) and *son* (village) were to be elected from among the assembly members, whereas mayors of *shi* (city) were appointed by the Minister of the Interior from a list of candidates provided by the assemblies. The cities' executives formed committees of councilors (e.g., mayors and deputy mayors). Through this significant reform, municipalities were given autonomous power at the local level regarding aspects of local life, such as family registers, public works, conscription, and elementary school management.

At this point, the national government began consolidating municipalities, known as the Great Meiji Consolidation. Initially, the municipalities, referred to as joint agricultural production units, survived by adopting the framework of a modern local government; however, because it was necessary to standardize the administration of some governmental systems, such as elementary schools, relatively small communities were compelled to change from what they had been for many decades. Consequently, the number of municipalities decreased to a little more than one-fifth of their original number, from 71,314 in 1888 to 15,859 in 1889.

One problem that arose during the merger process concerned the transfers of town and village properties. The rural villagers jointly owned and used hills and wastelands.

During the consolidation, the central government mandated that these properties should not be transferred to the new municipalities and that either the pre-merger communities should retain their customary rights or the newly established property wards (whose boundaries usually were identical to the old communities' boundaries) should get them. The intention was to protect traditional property rights. Because of this reform, the central focus among the residents living in the old consolidated villages was the ownership their former properties, even after consolidation, which delayed the harmonious formation of the identities of the newly formed municipalities. The municipalities were expected to discharge their responsibilities as governments. The Meiji Consolidation movement is considered the turning point from the "natural village" to the "administrative village" (Figure 2.1), and from that point, communities seem to have been treated more like the administrative units[1] that have been observed in other countries. After the Meiji Consolidation, Japan conducted two more consolidation movements.[2]

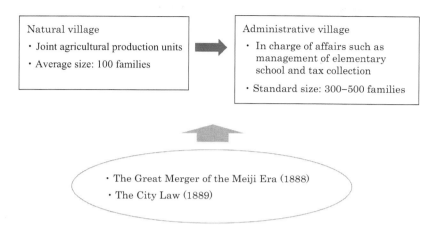

Figure 2.1 The process from natural village to administrative village
Source: Created by the author.

The Imperial Constitution was promulgated in 1889 and put into effect in 1890. The period between the 1890s and the 1920s was a progressive time for local governments under the Imperial Constitution. The central government extended suffrage and eligibility to serve in public office to all men aged 20 or older. The prefectures were permitted to enact regulations in 1929. On the other hand, the *gun* (county) was increasingly regarded as unnecessary to local government and it was eliminated in 1926. After 1929, preoccupation with World War II prompted many emergency measures, and the centralization of administrative functions deprived the local governments of the right of self-government.

The restructuring period (post–World War II era)

Japan's defeat in World War II in 1945 resulted in a complete revision of the national and local governmental systems, in which the existing laws regarding local governance were eliminated. The first stage of the reform began in 1946 when a new democratic constitution, the Constitution of Japan, was adopted and implemented on May 3, 1947. That same day, the Local Autonomy Law (LAL) went into effect; this law embodies the primary constitutional principle of local autonomy.

The restructuring of local governments was carried out from this point until the early 1950s. The Police Law, the Fire Defense Organization Law, and the Education Committee Law, all introduced between 1947 and 1948, transferred the responsibilities regarding policing, fire defense and protection, and education – previously tasks of the central government – to the local jurisdictions. Demands for a more rational local government led to the Municipal Merger Promotion Law in 1953. Under this law, a full-scale consolidation occurred, referred to as the Great Showa Consolidation, which decreased the number of municipalities by more than one-third (from 9,868 to 3,975) over three years. The economic growth of the 1960s was caused by industrial and population concentration in the large cities. On the other hand, the deserted countryside became a major domestic problem. There was a simultaneous need for the regional administration, including municipalities, which led to the formation of the regional administrative zone (RAZ) to address the demands of daily life in the urban and rural areas after 1969.

The period of maturation (post-1970s)

The 1973 oil crisis marked the end of the rapid and strong economic growth of the 1960s, and the rate of growth continued to slow down after 1975. The slow growth negatively influenced national and local public finances, and the various governments issued a massive amount of public bonds to combat their fiscal deficits, which instigated a further deterioration of Japan's financial structure. The economy recovered from the consequent recession in the late 1980s because of increasing asset prices, by which Japan entered an economic boom. Under those favorable conditions, the local governments shifted their uniform policies to individual policies that were more satisfying and created regional diversity.

In the 1990s, Japan entered a recession after the economic bubble burst, exposing all the structural problems that had accumulated since the end of World War II, including problems in the local governmental systems. Moderate and interim measures to decentralize had slowly been underway; however, a political coalition of various parties that was in place since 1993 made structural decentralization reform a major governmental and parliamentary issue. In 1995, the Decentralization Promotion Law was enacted.

Moreover, the sizes of local governments were also examined. Reinforcement of municipal cooperation was accomplished by revising the Local Autonomy Law in 1994, making it possible to create wide-area (regional) unions, and revision of the Municipal Merger Special Measures Law in 1995 introduced joint councils for mergers. Fiscal assistance for mergers was fortified in 1999, and the central government promoted municipal mergers. All of these measures were part of the Great Heisei Consolidation.

Therefore, municipal consolidations were successfully promoted throughout the country, and the 3,232 municipalities that existed in 1999 shrank to

1,717 in 2010. The central government ended municipal mergers in March of 2010, at which time the prefectures and municipalities entered a period of stability, with individual entities pursuing effective governance and fiscal health through administrative reform. Thus, the social, political, and economic changes and circumstances necessitated major reforms of Japan's local governments. It is essential to formulate appropriate responsibilities and delegate authority to the local governments that correspond to their individual situations and contexts.

The constitutional framework

Outline of the constitution

The first step of post–World War II democratic reform was to establish a new constitution, which was promulgated in 1946. Today's basic structure of local autonomy is based on this constitution. The constitution, in accord with the idea that local autonomy is requisite in a democratic society, situates local governments in the national framework and guarantees their autonomy. Chapter 8 of the constitution stipulated in four articles that local autonomy was to be guaranteed, as follows:

> ***Article 92.*** **Regulations concerning organization and operations of local public entities shall be fixed by law in accordance with the principle of local autonomy.**

Article 92 sets forth the basic "principle of local autonomy." This article is fundamental because the notion of local autonomy is believed to comprise two principles: autonomy of local government and autonomy of citizens. The former asserts the freedom of local government from the control of the central government, whereas the latter focuses on the self-administration of local authorities by citizens under their jurisdiction.

> ***Article 93.*** **The local public entities shall establish assemblies as their deliberative organs, in accordance with law.**
> **(2) The chief executive officers of all local public entities, the members of their assemblies, and such other local officials as may be determined by law shall be elected by direct popular vote within their several communities.**

Article 93 establishes the assembly and the public election of assembly members and chief executive officers autonomously by the relevant citizens. This article sets forth the most important elements of autonomy by residents, stating that the decisions made by local governments are in the hands of assemblies directly elected by residents, and the chief executive officers as well as the assembly members are to be elected directly by the residents. The elements of "the local public entities" are determined by the LAL, which was enacted in 1947. The LAL determines several types of local governments; the ones that are guaranteed by the constitution with respect to the daily lives of citizens are the prefectures and municipalities.

> **Article 94.** Local public entities shall have the right to manage their property, affairs and administration and to enact their own bylaws within law.

Article 94 confers administrative power to local governments and the autonomous right of legislative power within the scope of law in light of their autonomy.

> **Article 95.** A special law, applicable only to one local public entity, cannot be enacted by the Diet without the consent of the majority of the voters of the local public entity concerned, obtained in accordance with law.

Article 95 requires citizens' ballots of enactment for special laws (Local Autonomy Special Acts) that apply to individual local governments. This framework was frequently used in the 1950s, when 16 local laws were enacted. Thus, the autonomy of the local governments and of the people in their jurisdictions is guaranteed by these constitutional articles.

LAL as the basic law

Article 92 of the constitution stipulates that "regulations concerning organization and operation of local governments shall be fixed by law." Numerous laws have been enacted based on this provision, the most important and basic of which is the LAL that was implemented concurrently with the constitution in 1947. The LAL is the foundation of matters pertaining to the organization and operation of local governments, regarding such things as the type of local government, power, citizens, parliament, chief executives, and financial affairs; it also sets forth the elements of the relationship between the national government and the local governments and the elements of the relationships among local governments.

The LAL has three main features:

1 It widens the responsibility and authority of local governments, with relatively more powers assigned to councils and relatively less central supervision.
2 It provides measures for consolidating democracy, such as public elections of councilors, governors, and mayors, and several types of recall mechanisms or citizen initiatives.
3 It promotes pluralism by establishing numerous administrative boards, such as educational boards and financial auditors.

In addition to the LAL, other laws relating to local autonomy have been enacted, such as the Local Public Employee Law, the Public Offices Election Law, the Local Finance Law, and the Local Tax Law.

The structure of Japan's local governments

In Japan, local governments are juridical governments distinct from private for-profit corporations. According to a popular theory, a local government as a juridical body has the following three components:

1 It is a corporation bounded within a specified area of a national territory.
2 Its membership is provided to the residents therein.
3 Its basic function is to control the public administration of its area for the benefit of the public.

Another clause is also relevant: the competence of the local governments must be based upon the right of autonomy as recognized by the central government, which ultimately means the supremacy of the state over the local governments.

The characteristics of Japan's local governments

Based on the constitutional structure, the characteristics of Japanese local governments can be summarized as follows.

A unitary state

Japan is not a federal state, but a unitary state.

Two-tier system

The sub-national governments comprise two tiers: prefecture (a regional governmental jurisdiction) and municipality (a local-area governmental jurisdiction). The two levels of government have different juridical characteristics.

Pluralism and direct public elections of administrators

All local governments have a head or chief executive, governor/mayor, and assembly, referred to as a pluralist system. Effective checks and balances among these governmental dimensions are expected to establish an absolutely democratic local government. Moreover, the chief executives and assembly members are directly elected by the residents as guaranteed by Article 93 of the constitution as described earlier. This structure is the basis of all of the local governmental checks and balance systems.

Presidential system

The parliamentary cabinet system exists at the national level, but the local governments do not have a parliamentary system. They follow the chief executive system, also known as the presidential system. In this system, a chief executive has the power to ensure the comprehensive integrity of all the affairs of the government under his or her control.

Authority to enact bylaws

Prefectures and municipalities have authority to enact bylaws (Article 94 of the constitution). These bylaws cannot conflict with national laws; therefore, a bylaw that is incompatible with the national law has no legal binding authority.

Financial autonomy

Every local government has the authority to tax residents through enacting bylaws regarding taxes, collecting taxes, and using tax revenue. Moreover, every local government can draw up and execute budgets. This is their authority of independent financial discretionary power, which is a basis of financial autonomy.

The classifications of local governments

Outline

In Japan, local governments are juridical entities under Article 2 of the LAL. There are two main types of local governments: ordinary governments and special governments (Figure 2.2).

Ordinary local governments

Ordinary local governments assume the main role in the local administration. Ordinary local governments are subject to the constitutional guarantee of local autonomy, and they are comprised of prefectures and municipalities. The current local autonomy system is a dual structure of prefectures, within which are numerous municipalities. Table 2.2 provides the numbers of prefectures and municipalities that are ordinary local governments, followed by a description of the characteristics and situations of prefectures and municipalities.

Prefectures

The prefectures (*To*, *Do*, *Fu*, and *Ken*) are regional local governmental jurisdictions that encompass municipalities. Currently, Japan has 47 prefectures. Tokyo Metropolitan is the only prefecture designated as *To*. Tokyo Metropolitan is the capital of Japan and differs from *Do, Fu*, and *Ken* in that the

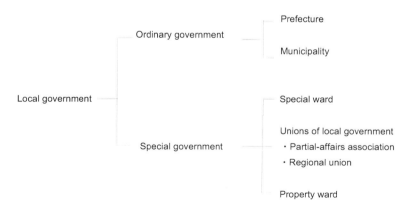

Figure 2.2 Classification of local governments
Source: Created by the author.

Table 2.2 Classification of ordinary local governments (as of April 1, 2015)

Ordinary Local Entities

Prefectures   47
    To (Tokyo Metropolitan)   1
    Do (Hokkaido)   1
    Fu (Osaka, Kyoto)   2
    Ken   43
Municipalities   1,718
    Shi (cities)   790
        Designated cities   20
        Core cities   45
        Exceptional cities at the time of the enforcement   39
    Cho (towns)   745
    Son (villages)   183

Special Local Entities

Special wards   23
Cooperatives of local authorities   1,630
    Wide-area unions (as of July 1, 2014)   115
    Partial cooperatives (as of July 1, 2014)   1,515
Community properties (as of April 1, 2012)   4,019
Local development corporation   1

Source: Created by the author using data from the Local Autonomy College.

latter are special wards. *Hokkaido* is the only prefecture designated as *Do*. *Kyoto* and *Osaka* are designated as *Fu*, and all others are designated as *Ken*. The differences among *Do, Fu*, and *Ken* are based on historical background; their governmental systems are identical. The populations and sizes (in km²) of the prefectures are shown in Table 2.3.

Table 2.3 shows the municipalities with their populations and sizes listed beneath their respective prefectures. Prefectures cannot exercise hierarchical or authoritarian power over them. Prefectures and municipalities have different roles in governance, and they must cooperate with each other as equals. The LAL sets forth prefectures' responsibilities in three categories (Article 2, the LAL):

1   The duty to cover a wider area than municipal territory;
2   The duty to require the cooperation and coordination of multiple municipalities;
3   The duty to manage matters not handled by ordinary municipalities after accounting for the scale and characteristics of such municipalities.

Table 2.3 Population and area by prefecture (as of October 1, 2010)

Prefecture	Population	Area (km²)	Capital/ Designated city
Hokkaido Area			
1. Hokkaido	5,506,419	83,456.87	● Sapporo
Tohoku Area			
2. Aomori	1,373,339	9,644.54	Aomori
3. Iwate	1,330,147	15,278.89	Morioka
4. Miyagi	2,348,165	7,285.76	● Sendai
5. Akita	1,085,997	11,636.25	Akita
6. Yamagata	1,168,924	9,323.46	Yamagata
7. Fukushima	2,029,064	13,782.75	Fukushima
Kanto Area			
8. Ibaraki	2,969,770	6,095.72	Mito
9. Tochigi	2,007,683	6,408.28	Utsunomiya
10. Gunma	2,008,068	6,363.33	Maebashi
11. Saitama	7,194,556	3,798.13	● Saitama
12. Chiba	6,216,289	5,156.70	● Chiba
13. Tokyo	13,159,388	2,187.50	
14. Kanagawa	9,048,331	2,415.86	● Yokohama
			● Sagamihara
			● Kawasaki
Hokuriku Area			
15. Niigata	2,374,450	12,583.81	● Niigata
16. Toyama	1,093,247	4,247.61	Toyama
17. Ishikawa	1,169,788	4,185.66	Kanazawa
18. Fukui	806,314	4,189.83	Fukui
Chubu-Tokai Area			
19. Yamanashi	863,075	4,465.37	Kofu
20. Nagano	2,152,449	13,562.23	Nagano
21. Gifu	2,080,773	10,621.17	Gifu
22. Shizuoka	3,765,007	7,780.42	● Shizuoka
			● Hamamatsu
23. Aichi	7,410,719	5,165.04	● Nagoya
24. Mie	1,854,724	5,777.27	Tsu

(*Continued*)

Table 2.3 (Continued)

Prefecture	Population	Area (km²)	Capital/ Designated city
Kinki Area			
25. Shiga	1,410,777	4,017.36	Otsu
26. Kyoto	2,636,092	4,613.21	◉ Kyoto
27. Osaka	8,865,245	1,898.47	◉ Osaka
			● Sakai
28. Hyogo	5,588,133	8,396.13	◉ Kobe
29. Nara	1,400,728	3,691.09	Nara
30. Wakayama	1,002,198	4,726.29	Wakayama
Chugoku Area			
31. Tottori	588,667	3,507.28	Tottori
32. Shimane	717,397	6,707.95	Matsue
33. Okayama	1,945,276	7,113.21	◉ Okayama
34. Hiroshima	2,860,750	8,479.58	◉ Hiroshima
35. Yamaguchi	1,451,338	6,113.95	Yamaguchi
Shikoku Area			
36. Tokushima	785,491	4,146.67	Tokushima
37. Kagawa	995,842	1,876.53	Takamatsu
38. Ehime	1,431,493	5,678.18	Matsuyama
39. Kochi	764,456	7,105.16	Kochi
Kyushu Area			
40. Fukuoka	5,071,968	4,977.24	◉ Fukuoka
			● Kitakyushu
41. Saga	849,788	2,439.65	Saga
42. Nagasaki	1,426,779	4,105.33	Nagasaki
43. Kumamoto	1,817,426	7,404.73	◉ Kumamoto
44. Oita	1,196,529	6,339.71	Oita
45. Miyazaki	1,135,233	7,735.99	Miyazaki
46. Kagoshima	1,706,242	9,188.78	Kagoshima
47. Okinawa	1,392,818	2,276.15	Naha

Source: Data from the Ministry of Internal Affairs and Communications (MIC).

○ Capital
◉ Designated city
● Other designated capital

Municipalities

OUTLINE

Municipalities are ordinary local governments involved in the affairs that matter most to the lives of the citizens. As of April 1, 2008, there were 1,788 municipalities (783 cities, 812 towns, and 193 villages) in Japan (Table 2.2). For municipalities to have the status of a city, certain requirements must be satisfied, such as a population of 50,000 or larger (the population requirement was 30,000 at the time of the Great Heisei Consolidation) and there must be an urbanized atmosphere. Towns and villages usually are designated as *gun*. However, *gun* is simply a geographical referent without administrative functions. Comparing towns to villages, towns have a more urbanized atmosphere and more people engaged in urban types of employment, such as commerce and industry, but the scope of affairs is similar between the two types of municipalities.

During the Great Heisei Consolidation, the number of cities increased and the number of towns and villages decreased. Cities are now proportionally the largest (46% of the total as designated cities, core cities, and other cities) (Figure 2.3).

DESIGNATED CITIES

Japan's large cities are ordinance-designated cities (designated cities). The LAL assumes that all cities with populations larger than 500,000 are designated by Cabinet order as designated cities. But the actual standard had been

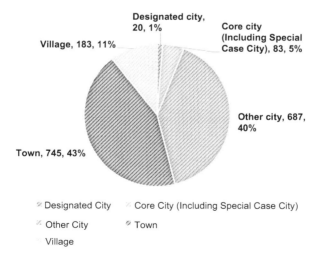

Figure 2.3 The classification of municipalities (as of January 2014)
Source: Created by the author using data from MIC.

reinforced to more than one million.[3] The designated cities are given extra legal authorities, such as the appointment of the faculty members, because they have large-scale organizations and high-level competences. Therefore the central government has kept the practical higher standard.

As of April 1, 2012, 20 cities qualified as designated cities (Table 2.4). Population size varies widely; the largest designated city is Yokohama city (nearly 3.7 million) and the smallest is Kumamoto city (about 734,000) (Figure 2.4).

Population growth also varies among the designated cities: Yokohama city, Nagoya city, and Sapporo city populations are increasing, whereas the other designated cities' populations are stable or slightly decreasing (Figure 2.5).

It is important to attend to the fact that the differences in size and growth are significant in this group of large cities.

Table 2.4 Designated cities (as of April 1, 2012)

City	Population (as of 2010)	Area (km²)	Designated date	Prefecture
Osaka	2,665,314	223	1956.9.1	Osaka
Nagoya	2,263,894	326.43	1956.9.1	Aichi
Kyoto	1,474,015	827.9	1956.9.1	Kyoto
Yokohama	3,688,773	437.57	1956.9.1	Kanagawa
Kobe	1,544,200	552.26	1956.9.1	Hyogo
Kitakyushu	976,846	489.6	1963.4.1	Fukuoka
Sapporo	1,913,545	1,121.12	1972.4.1	Hokkaido
Kawasaki	1,425,512	142.7	1972.4.1	Kanagawa
Fukuoka	1,463,743	341.7	1972.4.1	Fukuoka
Hiroshima	1,173,843	905.41	1980.4.1	Hiroshima
Sendai	1,045,986	785.85	1989.4.1	Miyagi
Chiba	961,749	272.08	1992.4.1	Chiba
Saitama	1,222,434	217.49	2003.4.1	Saitama
Shizuoka	716,197	1,411.93	2005.4.1	Shizuoka
Sakai	841,966	149.99	2006.4.1	Osaka
Niigata	811,901	726.1	2007.4.1	Niigata
Hamamatsu	800,866	1,558.04	2007.4.1	Shizuoka
Okayama	709,584	789.92	2009.4.1	Okayama
Sagamihara	717,544	328.83	2010.4.1	Kanagawa
Kumamoto	734,474	389.54	2012.4.1	Kumamoto

Source: Created by the author using data from MIC.

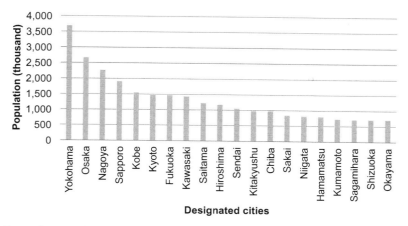

Figure 2.4 Population sizes of the designated cities

Source: Created by the author using data from MIC.

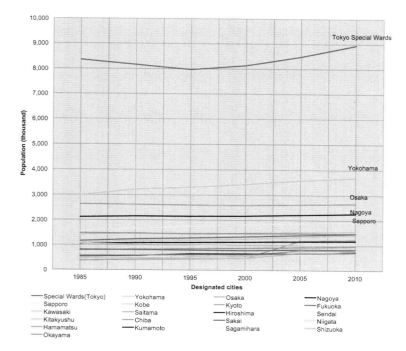

Figure 2.5 Population change by the designated cities

Source: Created by the author using data from MIC.

Designated cities are an exception to the rule of separation between prefectures and municipalities. They are permitted to conduct all or some of the functions normally carried out by prefectures regarding some administrative tasks, such as child welfare, welfare of people with mental disorders or physical handicaps, livelihood relief, and city planning. Designated cities also have power in areas such as the management of national roads and compulsory education, by enacting separate laws.

Tokyo Metropolitan District continues to economically grow (Figure 2.6).

Disparities of economic growth exist among the designated cities, as do growth rates. The size of Osaka city's gross product is much larger than those of the other designated cities but its growth has slowed. On the other hand, the gross product of Yokohama city has been growing among the designated cities (Figure 2.7).

CORE CITIES

Cities with populations larger than 200,000 are designated by Cabinet order as core cities. This designation was introduced in 1994 to provide cities smaller than designated cities with limited prefectural authority (Article 252-22, the LAL). As of April 1, 2015, 83 cities were designated as core cities. Core cities are allowed to conduct all or some of the functions delegated to designated cities, except for functions that are inappropriate for core cities or functions that can be more efficiently conducted by prefectures regarding

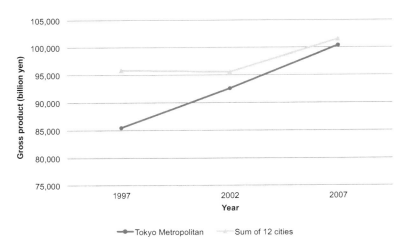

Figure 2.6 Change to gross products of listed cities, 1997–2007

Source: Created by the author using data from MIC.

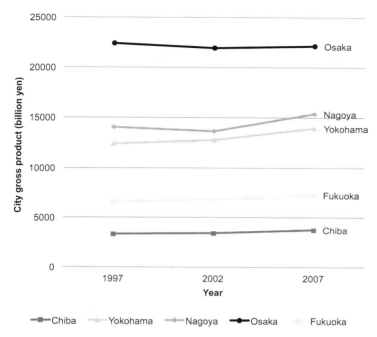

Figure 2.7 Change to some designated cities' gross products
Source: Created by the author using data from MIC.

public health centers, public welfare administration, city planning, and environmental conservation.

The designation of exceptional city was introduced in 2000 for cities that are smaller than core cities, and they are given some prefectural authority, although to quite a limited extent. The main criterion of this designation was that the city had a population no larger than 200,000. Before the 2014 amendment to the LAL, core cities (populations larger than 300,000) and special cities (populations larger than 200,000) were the only types of moderately large cities. However, as the transition of power to the local governments (decentralization) advanced, the differences between those two groups shrank, and the LAL amendments merged them together into the new designation of core cities.[4]

Special local governments

Special local governments are referred to as special because their missions are finite or their establishments are under special circumstances. Therefore their regions, structures, and authorities are particular and their existence is not universal. The LAL establishes three types of special local governments: special wards, unions, and property wards.

Special wards

Currently, there are 23 special wards: Chiyoda Ward, Shinjuku Ward, and so on. All of them are located in Tokyo Metropolitan. The administrative scope of special wards is slightly narrower than that of ordinary cities; however, their functions are almost identical. The main differences from ordinary cities are that Tokyo Metropolitan handles fire services, water supplies, sewage, and other services. It is assumed that those services are effectively managed in a unified way through the advantages of economies of scale because Tokyo has a population of more than 13 million (Table 2.1). The head and members of ward parliaments in the special wards are directly elected through public elections.

Unions of local governments

A union of local governments is an organization of two or more local governments to manage a particular service or problem when that problem would be more efficiently and reasonably handled by a union than by the individual governments.

There are two types of unions of local governments: partial-affairs associations (PAAs) and regional unions.

PARTIAL-AFFAIRS ASSOCIATIONS

PAAs are organizations among prefectures, municipalities, and/or special wards to jointly administer some functions. PAAs are established to handle services, such as garbage disposal and fire prevention (Chap. 2, V5, Table 2.6).

REGIONAL UNIONS

Regional unions are organizations established by prefectures, municipalities, or special wards to devise and execute comprehensive plans over a large geographic area with respect to functions that are deemed more comprehensively and systematically suited to an integrated approach over a large area (Chap. 2, V3, Table 3.5).

Property wards

Property wards are special local administrations established to manage a municipality's properties or facilities. They are local administrators established solely to manage properties, and many of them exist in agricultural or mountain villages. The most common of these properties are mountain forests, although some others are irrigation ditches, marshes, burial grounds, housing lots, paddies and fields, hot springs, and so on (Figure 2.2).

Two-tier system of local government

Basic classification

Two criteria are used to determine Japan's structure of local government. The first criterion is the principle of the unitary state versus the federal state. A unitary state is a state governed as a unit where the national government is the supreme authority and any sub-national entities have only those powers that the national government delegates to them. On the other hand, a federal state is a territorial and constitutional community that forms a federal union. It differs from a unitary state in that the affiliated entities of a federal state have transferred some of their sovereign powers to the federal government.

The second distinction is in the features of local governance. There is the Anglo-American type and the Continental type. The Anglo-American type has two basic characteristics:

1 Diversity across local governments' methods and structures.
2 Relatively advanced citizen participation, with mechanisms such as town meetings, recalls, and referenda.

On the other hand, the Continental type is characterized by:

1 The unity of local administrative rules is generally secured by national laws.
2 Sub-national entities have extensive power, but the national government retains substantial controls.

By combining these features, four classes can be devised as a typography, and Japan can be categorized as a unitary state of the Continental type (Table 2.5). This basic classification matters to the detailed rules that guide Japan's local governments.

Table 2.5 Frame of domestic administrative system

Types	Unitary State	Federal State
Anglo-American type	UK	US
Continental type	French Republic Japan	Federal Republic of Germany

Source: Created by the author.

Japan's case

Unitary state

As described earlier, since it began to progress as a modern state in the 1870s, Japan has had a unitary state system. In 1947, after World War II, Japan formulated its current constitution, which does not specifically create a unitary state. However, it sets forth the legislative powers vested in the Diet, which is the most powerful state body and the nation's only lawmaking body. The judiciary branch of government comprises the Supreme Court and the lower national courts. In this constitutional framework, the legislative powers to enact state laws would not be given to prefectural or municipal governments. Hence, the unitary system took root in Japan.

Two-tier system

Under the constitution, the LAL created the two-tier system of ordinary local governments. The number of tiers was influenced by numerous factors in the counties, such as population size, geographic features, extent of centralization, and historical backgrounds. In Japan, the previous incarnation of local governments comprised the *han* (clan) and the villages, which was a natural two-tier system. Moreover, some of Japan's characteristic features, such as population size and density, and its relatively strong centralization (before the 2000s), are believed to have been harmonious with the two-tier system.

Japan's local autonomy system adopted the two-tier system of prefectures (as regional governments) and municipalities (as basic local governments). The LAL provides that the municipalities, as basic local governments, manage most of the local affairs, except for those devolved upon prefectures by the LAL. This idea reflects the philosophy of decentralization and the principle of subsidiaries. This principle holds that social problems should be solved at the most immediate local level consistent with their solutions. Consequently, matters that are closely related to residents' daily lives are handled at the lowest level of local government. In other words, central authorities should have subsidiary functions, performing only those tasks that cannot be performed effectively at a more immediate or local level.[5]

Considering the number of tiers of administrative units in various countries, in the case of countries with a federal system, a four-tier pattern is standard: federation, state, wide-area local government, and basic local government. In the case of the unitary state, a three-tier pattern is standard: state, wide-area local government, and basic local government. Japan's system is the standard pattern of a unitary state.

Comparative analysis

The classifications presented in Table 2.6 compare the local governmental structures of countries.

It is important to pay attention to the relevant information about basic local governments. France, the US, and Germany historically have had many local governments. We can assume that smaller governments have desired to finely tune the public services in those countries. On the other hand, the UK has relatively fewer local governments, achieved through local reforms. Therefore, population per governmental unit (jurisdiction) in the UK (153,200) is much larger than in the other countries.

Japan's population per unit has increased (73,100), which is relatively close to that of the UK, because of the recent Great Heisei Consolidation. Thus, the UK and Japan have relatively large basic local governments. When local governments are compared across countries and cultures, these facts should be considered.

Allocation of affairs between prefectures and municipalities

Comprehensive power

Japan's local autonomy system does not apply a restrictive confining principle to the powers of local governments;[6] it uses the comprehensive authorizing principle. In other words, the LAL provides that the ordinary governments deal with their responsibilities in their region, and confers comprehensive power, that is, the general power on prefectures and municipalities legally designated as ordinary local governments. By using their general powers in addition to the specific powers authorized by laws, prefectures and municipalities act as comprehensive administrative entities in ways that are considered necessary to the citizens in their jurisdictions.

Relationship between prefectures and municipalities

Prefectures and municipalities are mutually independent local governments, and there is no hierarchical relationship in terms of their systems. However, the differences in their characters create differences in their functions. Whereas prefectures are regional governments that encompass

Table 2.6 Comparison of countries

Item	US	UK	France	Germany	Italy	Japan
style	Federal	Singular nation	Singular nation	Federal	Singular nation	Singular nation
Tier of local government unit	[State + two tiers (or one tier)] County Municipality	(England) [parallel; two tiers • single tier (two tiers) County – district (single tier) Unitary (Scotland, Wales, Northern Ireland) [single tier; autonomous government]	[Three tiers] Région Département Commune	[Land + Two tiers (parallel; Kreis-freie Stadt)] Kreis Gemeinde (parallel; Kreis-freie Stadt)]	[Three tiers] Regime Provincia Commune	[Two tiers] Prefecture Municipality
Number of basic local public entity (2011)	Municipality 19,519 (2012)	Local authority 406	Commune 36,682	Gemeinde, Kreis-freie Stadt 12,104	Commune 8,094	Municipality 1,749
Population (thousand)	313,874	62,195	64,812	81,744	60,468	127,799
Population per unit (thousand simple average)	16.1	153.2	1.8	6.8	7.5	73.1
Main affairs of basic local government	Education, police, health, welfare, road, firefighting, water and sewerage, transport	(Single tier) local plan, regulation of development, housing, environment sanitation, social welfare	Elementary school, kindergarten, childcare center, city planning, road, waste collection, cleaning	Schoolhouse (building/ maintenance), sewage, waste disposal, livelihood assistance	Social welfare, health, public works, vocational education	Social welfare, health, operation of elementary/ junior high school, road, firefighting
Main cooperate systems	Special district School district	Combined authority Joint board	SIVU Métropole	Ober Regionale-gemeindeverland Amt/Samt Gemeinde	Unione di comuni Comunità montane	Cooperation association

Source: Created by the author.

municipalities, municipalities are basic local governments closely related to their citizens' daily lives. Furthermore, prefectures advise municipalities on various matters from a regional perspective.

Characteristics

Under the LAL, prefectures, as regional governments, are defined to be the jurisdictions that comprehend the municipalities, and they manage regional affairs, communications, and coordination relating to municipalities as well as supplementing municipalities' efforts.

On the other hand, municipalities, as basic local governments, have roles regarding matters that are not dealt with by their prefectures. This organization reflects the principle of priority on municipalities. The principle regarding the allocation of responsibilities means that the responsibility and performance of matters should first be allocated to the municipalities and followed by prefectures. Matters that cannot be handled by either level of government should be handled by the state. This is the same idea as the principle of subsidiary.

However, in the actual allocation of responsibilities among the central, prefectural, and municipal governments, the allocation is not accomplished by allocating each type of affair; affairs of the same type are, in many cases, functionally borne at each stage.

For example, the central government, prefectures, and municipalities all have some responsibilities for Japan's educational system. In other words, the allocation of responsibilities is not of the separation type; it is the fusion type in Japan's local autonomy system.

Responsibilities held by prefectures and municipalities

Responsibilities held by prefectures

Responsibilities held by prefectures are as follows:

1 Regional affairs (e.g., maintenance of national roads, construction of prefectural roads, management of harbors, conservancy of forests and rivers, public health centers, vocational training, police);
2 Communication and coordination affairs related to municipalities (e.g., advice and recommendations, guidance for rationalizing the organization and operation of municipalities);
3 Supplement the affairs of municipalities (e.g., high schools, hospitals, public universities, museums).

Responsibilities held by municipalities

Responsibilities held by municipalities are as follows:

1   Affairs related to the basics of residents' lives (e.g., citizen registrations, family registers, citizen indicators);
2   Affairs related to ensuring the safety and health of citizens (e.g., fire services, garbage disposal, water supplies, sewage);
3   Affairs related to the welfare of citizens (e.g., nursing insurance, national health insurance, public assistance [within cities' limits]);
4   Affairs related to the urban development plan (e.g., urban design, city parks, municipal roads);
5   Affairs related to the establishment and management of facilities (e.g., elementary and junior high schools, libraries, daycare facilities, public halls, citizens' halls).

The major responsibilities allocated at the three governmental levels are summarized in Table 2.7.

Allocation of authority among municipalities

Population sizes are remarkably diverse among the municipalities: the largest jurisdiction is Yokohama city, with nearly 3.8 million residents, and the smallest jurisdiction is Aogashima village, with just 165 residents (both as of 2010). Therefore, the sizes of the organizational structure of the municipal governments differ according to population size. The LAL recognized this diversity and allocates authorities and the relevant individual laws with respect to the organizational sizes (Table 2.7).

The town/village is the smallest of the municipalities, and they are provided with the basic authorities of municipalities. Because they are so small, they do not have the authority to manage public livelihood assistance services; their prefectures are responsible for that service.

The city, sometimes referred to as the general city, is the second smallest jurisdiction and it has standard authority over the citizens' daily lives. Core cities are larger jurisdictions, with relatively more authority over such matters as operating healthcare centers, permitting catering establishments, and approving construction of elderly nursing homes. The designated cities constitute the largest group, currently numbering 20, including Yokohama city, Osaka city, Nagoya city, and Sapporo city. Designated cities have authority comparable to prefectures regarding, for example, the management of national/prefectural roads and appointment/dismissal of elementary and

Table 2.7 Allocation of responsibilities among the three levels of government

	Basic, Safety	Education	Welfare, Sanitation	Social infrastructure	Industry, Economy
Central	• Diplomacy • Defense • Judicature • Criminal punishment	• University • Subsidy for private school (university)	• Pension • Social insurance • License for doctor • Approval of medicine	• Highway • National road (designated section) • First-class river • Airport	• Currency • Banking regulation • Customs • Regulation on transportation • Regulation on Telecommunication • Economic policy
Local prefecture	• Police	• High school • Salary / Personnel of Elementary / junior high school • Subsidy for private school (others) • Sports facility • Cultural facility	• Livelihood assistance (area of town / village) • Child welfare • Elderly welfare • Health center	• National road (other section) • Prefecture road • First-class river (designated section) • Second-class river • Port • Public housing • Urban planning	• Vocational training • Support for small businesses
Municipality	• Fire defense • Family register • Resident register	• Elementary / junior high school • Kindergarten • Sports facility • Cultural facility	• Livelihood assistance (city) • Child welfare • Elderly welfare • Nursery care insurance • National health insurance • Water supply • Sewerage • Waste disposal • Health center (specific city)	• Municipal road • Small river • Port • Public housing	• Regulation on agricultural land use

Source: Data from MIC.

Item	Town/Village	City	Core City (Including Special Case City)	Designated City
Number	928	687	83	20
Authority of Prefecture				(Main) • Management of national/prefectural roads • Appointment/dismissal of teachers of elementary/junior high schools
			(Main) • Operating Healthcare Center • Permission of catering establishments • Approval of construction of elderly nursing home • Issue of physical disability handbook • Orders to industrial waste disposers • Approval of development with inurbanized area	
Authority of Municipality	• Public Livelihood Assistance	(Main) • Basic Resident Register • Family Register • Elderly Welfare • Child Welfare • Elementary/Junior High School • Waste Collection/Disposal • Water Supply/Sewage • Fire-fighting		

Figure 2.8 The structure of allocation of authority among municipalities, April 2014

Source: The materials of MIC.

Note: Special case cities were merged into core cities on April 1, 2015; the data on core cities reflect the core cities plus the special case cities.

junior high school teachers. Thus, there is a gradual increase in the amount of authority that is designed to maintain a balance between the functions and the organization control of local governments (Figure 2.8).

The financial aspects of the allocation of authority

The prefectures and municipalities manage many public functions in Japan. In other words, the responsibilities discharged by local governments cover all their internal administrative needs except for matters of diplomacy, defense, currency, and justice, which are managed by the national

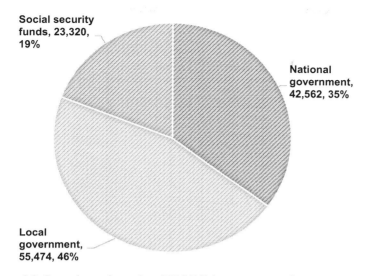

Social security funds, 23,320, 19%

National government, 42,562, 35%

Local government, 55,474, 46%

Figure 2.9 Gross domestic product (FY 2013) by governmental sector

Source: Created by the author using data from MIC: "*White paper on local public finance, 2015.*"

government. Therefore, Japan's local governments have extensive budgets requiring significant amounts of money. On the basis of final disbursements, the amount required by all of local (prefecture and municipality) governments exceeds that of the national government. In fiscal year (FY) 2013, the total local government gross domestic product (GDP) was about JPY 56 trillion (45.4% of overall GDP), whereas the national GDP was JPY 42 trillion (34.9% of overall GDP) (Figure 2.9).

The breakdown of expenditures reveals the nature of local public services (Figure 2.10). For example, among the governmental expenditures, public welfare (20.2%) and educational (8.8%) expenses are high. For both items, the share of local government is remarkably high: 72% for public welfare and 87% for education. With respect to these two expenditures, local governments have played the vital part in the internal administrative affairs to date.

Structures of the local government

Outline

Japanese local governments work under the principle of dual representation. This principle means that the assemblies and the chief executive officers of

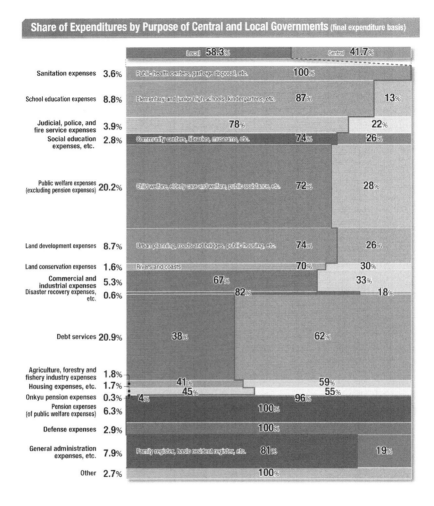

Figure 2.10 Share of expenditures by function of the local and national governments
        (Settlements, FY 2013)

Source: "White paper on local public finance, 2015."

the local governments are publicly elected as representatives by the residents of their jurisdictions. The presidential system is characterized by a checks and balances system, in which obvious checks are built into the relationship between the chief executive officer and the assembly. "All of these laws were passed during the Occupation, and each of them was designed to attack the previous system of centralization."[7]

These were times when deep conflict arose because the representatives of the two systems had different ways of thinking. Because tensions still tend to occur between the two levels of government, a cooperative style of management within local governments has evolved. Based on the characteristics of the dual representation system, mechanisms of control were built into the relationship of the assembly and the chief executive officer. In other words, the assembly and the chief executive officer have means by which they can engage checks and balances. Figure 2.11 shows the relationship between the two types of representatives.

Assembly

The assembly and the chief executive officer use numerous mechanisms when they make administrative decisions regarding local public agencies. The assembly has numerous ways to take initiative in policy making, as described in the following sections.

ASSEMBLY RESOLUTIONS

The foundation of assemblies' authority is in access to resolutions. Matters relating to assembly resolutions are organized into 15 categories stipulated in Article 96(1) of the LAL (as shown in Table 2.8). A local government administration also can present assembly resolutions by means of a bylaw (Article 96(2)) to expand the scope of an existing policy covered by a resolution.

RIGHT TO SUBMIT THE BILLS

Assembly members can submit bills to the assembly on any matter for which an assembly resolution is required (Article 112(1)). The assembly has a comparable mechanism for taking initiative in this regard. The difference between assemblies and chief executive officers is that assemblies have no authority to submit bills regarding budgetary matters.

INVESTIGATIVE AUTHORITY (PARTICULARLY UNDER ARTICLE 100 OF THE LAL)

Any of the duties of a local government may be investigated by its assembly. An assembly can call upon the relevant person for verbal or written testimony. This authority is referred to as investigative authority under Article 100, LAL. When testimony is requested on the basis of Article 100, the assembly must follow the same procedures and rules that would apply when questioning a witness in civil court. Furthermore, under Article 100, when people are asked to appear or give testimonies, those who decline or provide false testimony are fined. Therefore, the investigative process is a highly

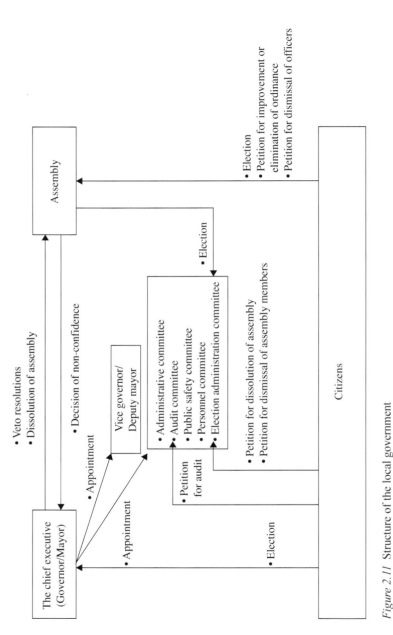

Figure 2.11 Structure of the local government

Source: Hitotsubashi Journal, *Law and Politics*, Vol. 42, "A multilayered check-and-balance system."

Table 2.8 Assembly resolution terms

1 Establishing, amending or abolishing bylaws.
2 Deciding budgets.
3 Approving statements of accounts.
4 Carrying out matters concerned with imposing or collecting local taxes and such.
5 Concluding contracts (respective sums of money and such).
6 Handling the transfer of property.
7 Investing property as a trust.
8 Dealing with the acquisition and disposal of various kinds of property and monetary amounts.
9 Receiving a donation with conditions attached.
10 Dealing with the renunciation of rights,
11 Making important public facilities set out for exclusive or long-term use.
12 Dealing with matters raised by a local public body, including demands, expressions of dissatisfaction, proposed lawsuits, negotiated settlement, mediation, and arbitration.
13 Deciding the amount of compensation for damages.
14 Comprehensive adjustment of activities carried out by public entities
15 In addition to the foregoing, all matters falling within the purview of an assembly as determined by laws or government orders based on these laws.

Source: Created by the author.

effective mechanism of the assembly that it can use to strengthen its position relative to the chief executive officer.

SUBMISSION OF A WRITTEN OPINION

Assemblies can submit written opinions on matters of public interest in the local jurisdiction to the National Diet or to an appropriate governmental agency. These opinions have no legal standing. However, the opinions cover a wide range of administrative areas and they are not limited to issues of local administration.

Opinions can be submitted on matters of diplomacy, national security issues, and other national level concerns. This mechanism is flexible, swift, and popularly used by many assemblies.

NON-CONFIDENCE

Non-confidence is an assembly's ultimate mechanism to resolve problems. In the event of an ongoing conflict, an assembly can obtain a vote of non-confidence. "Normally the resolution of no confidence is of course the assembly's ultimate weapon to resolve its conflicts with the executive."[8] Such a vote requires a quorum of at least two-thirds of the assembly members and the motion must pass with at least three-fourths of the assembly. If an assembly passes a non-confidence resolution and the chief executive officer does not dissolve the assembly within 10 days, the chief executive officer automatically loses his or her office. The assembly takes the risk of being dissolved, but if it successfully passes a non-confidence resolution, it has politically lethal leverage on the chief executive.

Chief executive

When making administrative decisions regarding public agencies, the chief executive uses the following mechanisms.

RIGHT TO SUBMIT BILLS

The right to submit bills is a basic right of chief executives as a way to initiate policy. These bills include bylaws, budgets, contracts, and others. Assembly members also have this right; however, chief executives have the exclusive right to submit bills on budgetary matters because chief executives are responsible for the sound financial management of the local governments, and as such have sole authority to control budgets. Budgets are central to policy initiatives, and therefore chief executives have significant power.

ATTENDANCE

Under the Article 121 of the LAL, chief executives shall appear to give testimony or explanations when asked by the assembly chairpersons. Article 121 is an obligatory measure aimed at chief executives, but it also represents an opportunity for chief executives to explain the bills that they have submitted. This communication covers the public as well as the assembly because speeches and other assembly proceedings are widely covered by newspaper, television, and Internet media. Attending assembly meetings are good opportunities for chief executives to move their initiatives forward.

RIGHT TO CONVENE THE ASSEMBLY ON PRINCIPLE

The right to convene an assembly is vested in the chief executive officer of the local government (Article 101(1)). The assembly holds regular and extraordinary sessions.

A regular session must be convened as specified by the relevant bylaws; usually, there are four sessions per year. An extraordinary session is convened to discuss specific agenda items when deemed necessary (Articles 102(1)–(3)). When an assembly chairperson requests a chief executive officer to convene an extraordinary session for a particular matter to be discussed, or when at least one-fourth of the assembly members make such a request, the chief executive officer must convene a session within 20 days.

This is a standard parliamentary procedure. This system is not common among countries with a presidential type of local governance; however, it is a way for the chief executive to steer the assembly.

A serious conflict between the chief executive and the assembly occurred in Akune city in 2010 when the mayor, the head of the chief executive, would not convene the assembly despite the requests of the assembly chairperson. The LAL was amended in 2012 to mitigate these types of problems. Post-amendment, the chairperson can convene extraordinary sessions in the face of refusal by the chief executive officer.

MEASURES THAT CHECK THE ASSEMBLY

Sometimes, serious conflicts arise because the assembly members and their chief executive officer have different views on policies. The central mechanisms of the dual representative system are the mechanisms that control and steer the relationship between the chief executive officer and the members of the assembly. The mechanisms that pertain to the assembly are:

1   The chief executive officer has the right to veto resolutions passed by the assembly and to seek its reconsideration of those resolutions.

    Vetoes can be general vetoes (ordinary reconsideration) or special vetoes (reconsideration of illegal resolutions or elections). General vetoes can be exercised by chief executive officers at his or her discretion when resolutions adopted by the assembly, revisions, or abolishment of bylaws or budgets are not desired. However, if at least two-thirds of the assembly votes a second time in favor of that resolution, it is adopted and cannot be vetoed. Special vetoes are provided as a way to avoid illegal acts and its exercise is mandatory for the chief executive officer.

2   Discretionary actions can be exercised by chief executive officers using powers normally held by the assembly under two conditions:

    a   when an assembly has not been convened and action is required on its behalf or when an assembly fails to act on a matter requiring its attention;
    b   when a right normally held by the assembly is exercised in accord with a prior agreement and the assembly delegates its authority in some minor matter to the chief executive to more efficiently carry out the government's responsibilities.

    When an assembly has not been convened and action is required, the chief executive officer can handle the matter when (1) an assembly is not duly formed; (2) an assembly is unable to open proceedings, particularly where there is an urgent need and insufficient time to obtain a quorum; or (3) an assembly does not pass a resolution on a matter on which it should pass a resolution (Article 179(1)). In these cases, the assembly must subsequently approve all discretionary actions. If that subsequent approval is not obtained, although the political responsibility falls on the chief executive officer, the validity of said discretionary action is not affected. This measure is very effective when urgent matters arise and a chief executive officer must act swiftly.

However, the measure has caused controversy in the past. In the Akune city in 2010 described earlier, a deputy mayor was appointed under this clause, which caused a reaction in the city and so much controversy that the LAL was amended in 2012 to eliminate the ability to appoint a vice governor or deputy mayor.

3   The right to dissolve the assembly as a countermeasure against a resolution of non-confidence.

In an ongoing conflict between the chief executive officer and the assembly that seems incapable of resolution, the assembly may pass a vote of non-confidence in the chief executive officer. A non-confidence vote requires a quorum of at least two-thirds to be presented and the motion must pass by at least three-fourths of the assembly.

If a non-confidence motion passes, the chief executive officer may in turn dissolve the assembly. This is a mechanism intended to resolve a deadlock between the chief executive officer and the assembly, through an appeal to the fair judgment of the voters. If the assembly passes a motion of non-confidence in the chief executive officer and the chief executive officer does not dissolve the assembly within the prescribed period (10 days), the chief executive automatically loses his or her position as the head of the government. Furthermore, if the assembly again passes a non-confidence motion at the first meeting convened after a dissolution, the chief executive cannot dissolve the assembly a second time and necessarily loses his or her position on the day that the second vote of non-confidence passes. The right to dissolve an assembly in a presidential system is exceptional. Chief executive officers can veto and they dissolve their assemblies at multiple levels of government.

System of checks and balances

Table 2.9 lists the rights of the chief executive officer and the assembly demonstrating the multilayered nature of the system of checks and balances.

Under the dual representative system, the chief executive officer and the assembly have a variety of mechanisms for implementing policy. The fact that both actors can exercise formal powers creates a power balance between them and enhances the transparency of the policy making process in local government.

Table 2.9 Checks and balances: chief executive and assembly

Chief Executive (Governor/Mayor)

1 Right to submit bills (including the exclusive right to submit bills on budgetary matters)
2 Attendance at the assembly and chance to explain the points of the bills and appealing the bills through Q and A at the assembly
3 Right to convene the assembly in principle
4 Veto
5 Discretionary action by the chief executive
6 Right to dissolve the assembly

Assembly

1 Assembly resolution (including increase and decrease budget amendment)
2 Right to submit the bills
3 Investigative authority (especially authority under Article 100 of Local Autonomy Law)
4 Submission of a written opinion
5 Non-confidence

Source: Created by the author.

However, some people point out that chief executive officers' mechanisms dominate those of the assembly. "The legislative record of most assemblies seems to indicate that the chief executive is still in a predominant position."[9] When one considers that the chief executive has both veto authority and the right to dissolve the assembly, this view has some merit. Each mechanism has important consequences and the fact that the chief executive has both powers is an internationally unique system.

Problems in the Japanese local governmental system

Japanese local government has confronted some problems. In this chapter, three problems are of particular interest: (1) diversity among local governments, (2) widening disparities, and (3) population flow into urban areas. In addition, the directional movement of local government is discussed.

Diversity among local governments

As of 2014, Japan had 47 prefectures and 1,718 municipalities, which are quite diverse regarding aspects of the population and geographic size.

Population

Figure 2.12 shows the size variation among the prefectures.

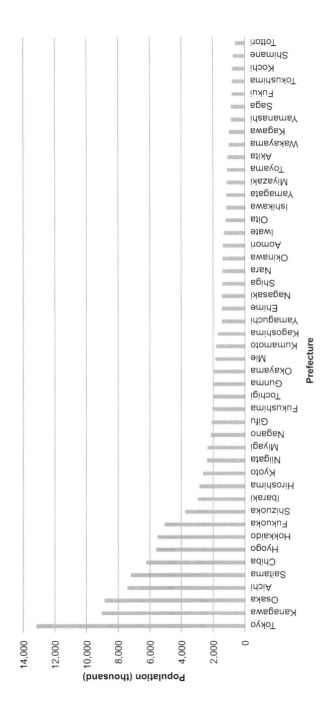

Figure 2.12 Populations of the prefectures (as of October 1, 2010)

Source: Created by the author using census data from MIC (see Table 1).

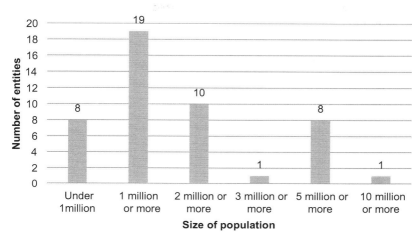

Figure 2.13 Distribution of prefectures by population size (as of October 1, 2010)
Source: Created by the author using census data from MIC.

The prefectures in the traditional industrial regions (Osaka, Aichi, Hyogo, and Fukuoka), those in metropolitan areas (Tokyo, Kanagawa, Saitama, and Chiba), and Hokkaido (largest in size) have large populations. These nine jurisdictions have populations in excess of five million (Figure 2.13).

On the other hand, in remote rural areas far from urban centers there are small prefectures with populations less than one million: Tottori, Shimane, Kochi, and so on. The largest jurisdiction is Tokyo, whose population is about 13 million, which is 22 times the size of Tottori prefecture, the smallest prefecture, with a population of 588,000. These salient differences are caused by factors such as natural conditions, administrative distinctions, and the extent of industrial concentration. These differences remain crucial issues for local governments.

Even among the cities there are great differences. There are 11 big cities with populations greater than one million; all of them are the designated cities. On the other hand, there are 75 small cities with populations less than 30,000 (Figure 2.14).

The smallest size group of municipality is towns and villages. Among them there are the lager entities whose populations are more than 50,000. The smaller entities' populations are under 1,000 (Figure 2.15).

Among the municipalities, the largest government is Yokohama city, with a population of about 3.8 million; this is about 22,000 times larger

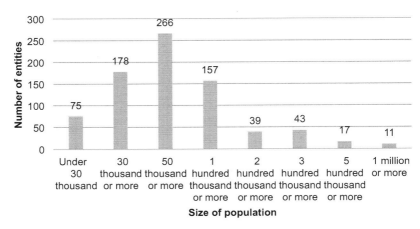

Figure 2.14 Distributional situation of cities by population size (as of October 1, 2010)
Source: Created by the author using census data from MIC.

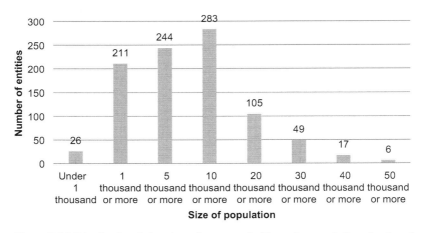

Figure 2.15 Distributional situation of towns and villages by population size (as of October 1, 2010)
Source: Created by the author using census data from MIC.

than the smallest municipality, Aogashima village, which has a population of just 190. The size of the municipality is affected by the natural situation and historic background, both of which account for the large disparity in sizes. All the municipalities are operated by the unified administrative structure commencing with LAL. However, the difference of population, size of finance, size of organization of entity and function are so huge that overcoming those gaps is not a simple matter.

Area

Distributional situations by area size are shown in Figure 2.16 for prefectures, Figure 2.17 for cities, and Figure 2.18 for towns and villages. Relatively numerous prefectures' area sizes are no fewer than 3,000 km² nor more than 5 km².

The area sizes of cities are more scattered than prefectures, towns, and villages. One factors is thought to be the great municipal annexations. Japan has experienced three great municipal annexations, as stated earlier, resulting in the establishment of new cities. The combination of annexation is diversified; multiple combinations of numbers of entities and area sizes exist. These annexations seem to exacerbate the scattered situation (Figure 2.17).

The area sizes of towns and villages are generally a little smaller than those of cities. There are numerous cities with area sizes around 100 km². On the other hand, there are numerous towns and villages with area sizes not more than 100 km² (Figure 2.18).

Based on these data, we can recognize that the Japanese local administration system is facing the issues not only of differences in population size but also of area size.

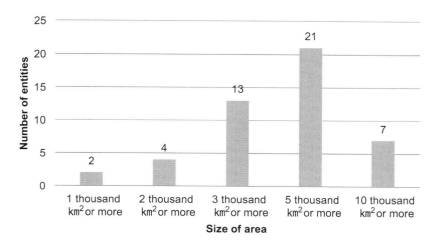

Figure 2.16 Distributional situation of prefectures by area size (as of October 1, 2010)
Source: Created by the author using census data from MIC.

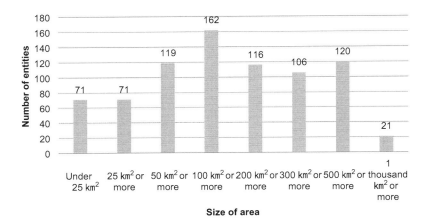

Figure 2.17 Distributional situation of cities by area size (as of October 1, 2010)
Source: Created by the author using census data from MIC.

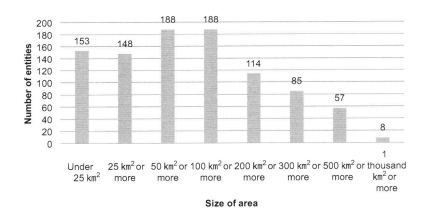

Figure 2.18 Distributional situation of towns and villages by area size (as of October 1, 2010)
Source: Created by the author using census data from MIC.

Widening disparities

On the premise of the differences among the local governments, the dispari-ties are widening. In this section we focus on the trend of prefectures and designated cities.

Prefectures

Focusing on the relation between population and increase-decrease ratio from 1990 to 2010 by prefecture, we find a certain correlation: the coefficient of correlation is .607 (Table 2.10 and Figure 2.19).

Table 2.10 Situation of population by prefecture

Prefecture	1990 (A) (thousand)	2010 (B) (thousand)	(B)/(A)×100(%)
Hokkaido	5,644	5,506	97.6
Aomori	1,483	1,373	92.6
Iwate	1,417	1,330	93.9
Miyagi	2,249	2,348	104.4
Akita	1,227	1,086	88.5
Yamagata	1,258	1,169	92.9
Fukushima	2,104	2,029	96.4
Ibaraki	2,845	2,970	104.4
Tochigi	1,935	2,008	103.8
Gumma	1,966	2,008	102.1
Saitama	6,405	7,195	112.3
Chiba	5,555	6,216	111.9
Tokyo	11,856	13,159	111.0
Kanagawa	7,980	9,048	113.4
Niigata	2,475	2,374	95.9
Toyama	1,120	1,093	97.6
Ishikawa	1,165	1,170	100.4
Fukui	824	806	97.8
Yamanashi	853	863	101.2
Nagano	2,157	2,152	99.8
Gifu	2,067	2,081	100.7
Shizuoka	3,671	3,765	102.6
Aichi	6,691	7,411	110.8
Mie	1,793	1,855	103.5
Shiga	1,222	1,411	115.5
Kyoto	2,602	2,636	101.3
Osaka	8,735	8,865	101.5
Hyogo	5,405	5,588	103.4
Nara	1,375	1,401	101.9
Wakayama	1,074	1,002	93.3
Tottori	616	589	95.6

(*Continued*)

Table 2.10 (Continued)

Prefecture	1990 (A) (thousand)	2010 (B) (thousand)	(B)/(A) × 100(%)
Shimane	781	717	91.8
Okayama	1,926	1,945	101.0
Hiroshima	2,850	2,861	100.4
Yamaguchi	1,573	1,451	92.2
Tokushima	832	785	94.4
Kagawa	1,023	996	97.4
Ehime	1,515	1,431	94.5
Kochi	825	764	92.6
Fukuoka	4,811	5,072	105.4
Saga	878	850	96.8
Nagasaki	1,563	1,427	91.3
Kumamoto	1,840	1,817	98.8
Oita	1,237	1,197	96.8
Miyazaki	1,169	1,135	97.1
Kagoshima	1,798	1,706	94.9
Okinawa	1,222	1,393	114.0

Source: Data from MIC.

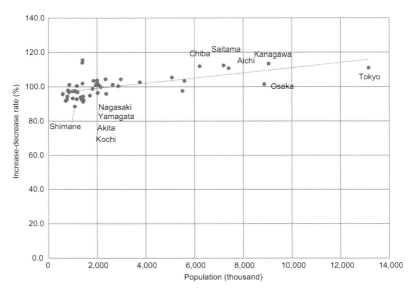

Figure 2.19 The correlation between population and increase-decrease ratio (2010/1990) (coefficient of correlation = .607)

Source: Created by the author using data from MIC.

This means that larger prefectures in terms of population grow at a greater rate. The traditional prefectures with large populations such as Tokyo, Kanagawa, Saitama, Chiba, and Aichi have a greater rate of population increase as shown in Figure 2.19.

When we examine the variance of population among the 47 prefectures, we see it has increased from 5,871,533 in 1990 to 7,193,982 in 2010 (Table 2.11).

These facts show that the disparity in population size among the prefectures have been widening.

Designated cities

Next we focus attention on the changes of population of 20 cities, the current designated cities. The designated cities are set down by the Cabinet orders. First, there are the traditional 10 large cities; they were provided by the order before 1981 and are listed at the top of Table 2.12. Then there are the 10

Table 2.11 Variance in prefecture population

Year	1990	2010
Variance	5,871,533	7,193,982

Source: Created by the author using data from MIC.

Table 2.12 Population changes in 20 cities (current designated cities)

	1985	*1990*	*1995*	*2000*	*2005*	*2010*
Yokohama	*2,993*	*3,220*	*3,307*	*3,427*	*3,580*	*3,689*
Nagoya	*2,116*	*2,155*	*2,152*	*2,172*	*2,215*	*2,264*
Kyoto	*1,479*	*1,461*	*1,463*	*1,468*	*1,475*	*1,474*
Osaka	*2,636*	*2,624*	*2,602*	*2,599*	*2,629*	*2,665*
Kobe	*1,411*	*1,477*	*1,424*	*1,493*	*1,525*	*1,544*
Kitakyushu	*1,056*	*1,026*	*1,020*	*1,011*	*994*	*977*
Sapporo	*1,543*	*1,672*	*1,757*	*1,822*	*1,880*	*1,914*
Kawasaki	*1,089*	*1,174*	*1,202*	*1,249*	*1,327*	*1,425*
Fukuoka	*1,160*	*1,237*	*1,284*	*1,341*	*1,401*	*1,464*
Hiroshima	*1,044*	*1,086*	*1,109*	*1,126*	*1,154*	*1,174*
Sendai	700	*918*	*971*	*1,008*	*1,025*	*1,046*
Chiba	789	829	857	887	*924*	*962*
Saitama	377	418	453	485	1,176	*1,222*

(*Continued*)

Table 2.12 (Continued)

	1985	1990	1995	2000	2005	2010
Shizuoka	468	472	474	470	701	*716*
Sakai	818	808	803	792	831	*842*
Niigata	476	486	495	501	785	*812*
Hamamatsu	514	535	562	582	804	*801*
Okayama	572	594	616	627	675	*710*
Sagamihara	483	532	571	606	629	*718*
Kumamoto	556	579	650	662	670	734
Total	22,280	23,303	23,772	24,328	26,400	27,153

Source: Created by the author using data from MIC.

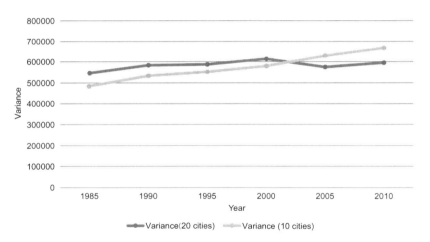

Figure 2.20 Change of variance of population among the designated cities

Source: Created by the author using data from MIC.

more recently added cities (e.g., Sendai city was set down in 1989). They are shown in the bottom column of Table 2.12. Numbers in italics show the populations following city designation.

We can see newly added cities experienced the expansion of the residents through annexation because the legal requirement was around one million residents and exceptionally more than 700,000 from 2001 to 2010. This is why the population variance among the 20 cities has been flattening out: the newly added cities have reached a population of more than 700,000.

On the other hand, when we focus on the traditional 10 cities, the variance of population among the cities increased (Figure 2.20).

Yokohama city, Nagoya city, and Sapporo city have continued the notable growth in population, but at the same time some cities show the decrease or flattening out (Figure 2.5).

Here we can see the fact that even the designated cities have demonstrated widening population disparities.

Population decline and inflow to urban area

Japan's population hit a peak in 2008 and has been declining since then (Figure 2.21).

This trend is thought to arise from a low birth rate. This is now such a high policy agenda that the national government and local governments have kept up their efforts to expand public support for childbirth, child-rearing, and other related policies.

However, the sharp decline in the population is a far more serious issue for provincial areas for big cities. Rates of population for prefectures show that the downtrend is more distinguished in provincial prefectures (Table 2.13 and Figure 2.22).

This phenomenon is thought to be attributed to population inflow to urban cities. The rural regions are affected by the double-barreled effects of low birthrate and outflow of residents commencing with the younger generation.

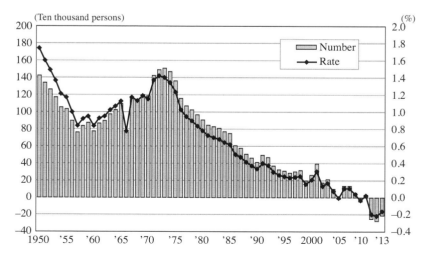

Figure 2.21 Number and rate of population change

Source: "Current population estimates as of October 1, 2013," Statistics Bureau, MIC.

Table 2.13 Rates of population change for prefectures

	Prefecture	Rates of population change
	Japan	−0.17
1	Tokyo	0.53
2	Okinawa	0.44
3	Aichi	0.21
4	Saitama	0.14
5	Kanagawa	0.13
⋮	⋮	⋮
43	Wakayama	−0.84
44	Kochi	−0.89
45	Yamagata	−0.90
46	Aomori	−1.04
47	Akita	−1.18

Source: Data from MIC.

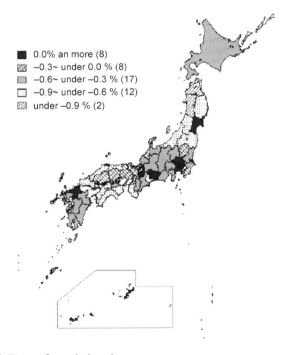

Legend:
- 0.0% an more (8)
- −0.3~ under 0.0 % (8)
- −0.6~ under −0.3 % (17)
- −0.9~ under −0.6 % (12)
- under −0.9 % (2)

Figure 2.22 Rates of population change

Source: Statistics Bureau, Ministry of Internal Affairs and Communications website (http://www.stat.go.jp/english/data/jinsui/2013np/index.htm).

Data shows the change of population of urban cities which are composed of Tokyo special wards and the designated cities. The number and the share of population of those urban cities have been consistently increasing (Figures 2.23 and 2.24).

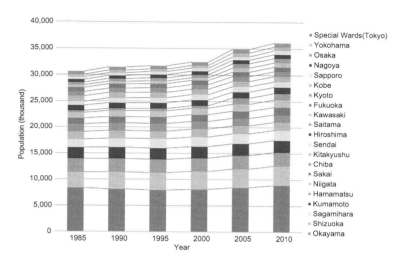

Figure 2.23 Change of population in urban cities

Source: Created by the author using data from MIC.

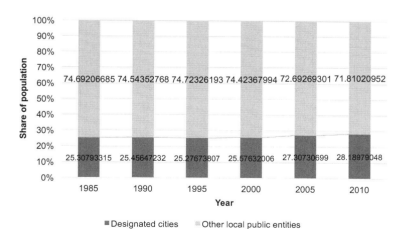

Figure 2.24 Change of share of population in urban cities

Source: Created by the author using data from MIC.

Nowadays one-third of Japanese live in the large cities whose populations are more than 700,000.

Conclusion

This chapter has presented an overview of the basic structure of the local government system and the current agenda for local governments. The local government system has been facing an extravagant difference in entity size, widening population disparities, the downtrend of community populations, the inflow to urban cities, and so forth.

Those issues may be common among the countries. However, the range of affairs of local government is so wide in Japan that those issues have been exerting strong influences on local administration.

Local governments have been making various ingenious plans for addressing these problems, and one of these important measures is wide-area administration methods. In the following chapters we shall focus on those systems.

Notes

1 For example, in France, a commune is often considered a socially strong cohesive unit.
2 The Great Showa Consolidation was conducted from 1953 to 1956 and the Great Heisei Consolidation was conducted from 1999 to 2010.
3 The cities that have populations greater than 800,000 and are expected to grow to be more than one million are included. Moreover, from 2001 to 2010 these regulations were reduced for the purpose of promoting the amalgamation.
4 The amendment was implemented on April 1, 2015. Before the merger, there were 43 core cities and 40 special cities.
5 This principle was a key element of the European Charter of Local Self-Government, an instrument of the Council of Europe promulgated in 1985.
6 In contrast, the local authorities in the UK have standing regarding restrictive enumerating powers.
7 Kurt Steiner, *Local Government in Japan* (California, 1965) 331.
8 Steiner, 369.
9 Steiner, 372.

3 The basic structure of Japan's wide-area (regional) governance

The requirement of local government[1]

What is the best size of local government to benefit the residents? Several social factors are involved. Theoretically, large governments have consistent positive influences in four major ways.

First, large local governments can provide relatively more administrative specialists, such as doctors, nurses, childcare workers, nutritionists, agricultural engineers, building engineers, civil engineers, and librarians. In this way, size is positively related to the administrative skill of the local government. Second, large local governments have larger tax bases and manage larger accounts and funds. In that sense, size is positively related to financial stability. Third, large local governments have relatively large populations of citizens and corporations that tend to comprise diverse individuals, families, and corporations, which tends to increase the political diversity of the government. Fourth, the scope of public projects and the sizes of the groups potentially influenced by policy are relatively large, which leads to social trust in the government.

On the other hand, there are several social factors related to a large government that would have negative effects. First, large governments tend to result in fewer close interpersonal relationships among neighbors in communities. Second, local attachments and subjective orientations are negatively affected by large size because a large government negatively influences social embeddedness. Third, concerning associational memberships, residents are less engaged in larger municipalities. These social factors negatively influence the competence of basic local government. However, citizens are expected to select a well-qualified size based on social preferences.

Considering the Japanese experience, at the promulgation of the Municipal Government Act in 1888, Japan instituted the administrative village. The local governments transitioned from the natural village to the

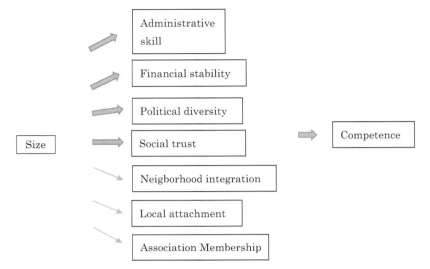

Figure 3.1 Relationship between size and political competence in local government

Source: Created by the author. In setting the social elements, "*Size and Local Democracy*" (Bas Denters et al., 2014) was used as a reference.

administrative village. The administrative village is believed to have been more favorable to the social factors that relate governmental size to positive outcomes. Moreover, under the requirements of national administrative modernizing in the twentieth century, and the responses to the flourishing of decentralization in the twenty-first century, the social situation seems relatively more conducive to the positive social factors (Figure 3.1).

Need for wide-area public services

The prefectures and municipalities (ordinary governments) are fully operational administrations that manage all of the administrative responsibilities allocated by national laws. However, as discussed in Chapter 2 (see Figure 2.10), local governments manage such a broad range of services that some services are not easily managed by an individual government's resources among its many other affairs. This is imperative in Japan's modern local governmental system. These types of matters are shown in Figure 3.2.

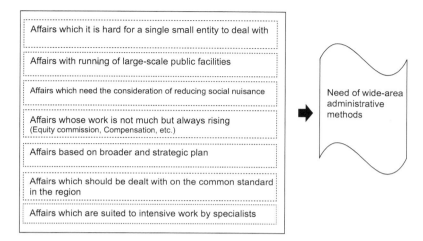

Figure 3.2 Need for regional administrative involvement
Source: Created by the author.

1   Services that are challenging for individual small governments to manage. Some services need regional administrative management and some
of them need significant clerical attention. Those matters are sometimes challenging for an individual small government to handle (e.g.,
regional development plans, medical care for the elderly, and forest
road maintenance).

2   Matters regarding the operation of large-scale facilities. Some services
require large public facilities that would be challenging for an individual small municipality to manage because of extensive construction and
maintenance costs (e.g., refuse disposal, crematoria, and sewage systems).

3   Matters regarding the reduction of social nuisances. Some activities
lead to nuisances, such as noise, ground pollution, and so on. For those
types of problems, cooperation among governments for nuisance abate-
ment is crucial (e.g., refuse disposal).

4   Activities of increasing volume. Although the extent of clerical work
regarding some activities may not initially be great, the potential of an
increasing volume of work exists. For those activities, sharing the administrative workload is reasonable (e.g., public workers' compensation,
retirement allowances for civil service workers, and equity commission).

5   Activities based on broad strategic plans. Some matters require consensus among relevant local governments in a regional unit (prefecture)
(e.g., broad area (regional) development plans).

6   Matters that should be handled using the common standard of a region. Some activities need to be managed in accord with the common administrative standards of a region (prefecture) (e.g., nursing insurance and elder care services).
7   Services that require the attention of specialists. Some matters and services need specialists, and the sharing of those human resources is a reasonable way to manage those matters (e.g., fire defense, emergency medical care, and welfare of handicapped people). For all of these matters, the regional administration is significantly required. This situation is a globally common phenomenon, and every country has local governments that are facing problems of regional administration. Wide-area administrative methods are imperative for effective and efficient public services.

What is the orientation of regional governance? In Japan, there have been two approaches. One approach has been consolidation, which has generally taken the form of consolidating (amalgamating) municipalities. The other option is the cooperation approach, meaning the cooperatives of the local governments. The local government can take the wide-area administrative methods: establishing partial-affairs associations (PAA), making the delegation of affairs, and so on (see Table 3.2 and Figure 3.3).

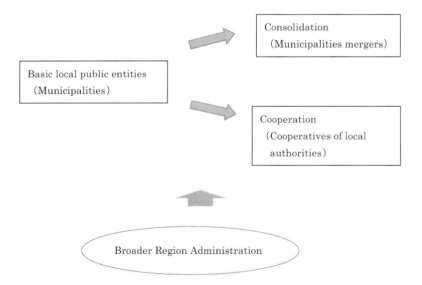

Figure 3.3 Regional governance
Source: Created by the author.

When a local government chooses to consolidate or cooperate, its decision is based on its preferred size for the local governmental administration. When a local government meets the needs of the regional public services, the local government that prefers a larger administration based on the relevant social factors would choose to consolidate (see Figures 3.1 and 3.3). When the local government prefers to maintain its present size, it chooses the cooperative approach. Figure 3.4 shows the change in the number of the local governments among Japan, France, Switzerland, and the US.

This figure demonstrates that the number of basic local governments in France (communes), the US (municipalities), and Switzerland (municipalities) have been quite stable. In France, there were 36,767 communes in 2014, which has been stable at about 36,000 since 1861. In the US, the number of municipalities has been stable at about 19,000. In Switzerland, the number of municipalities decreased from about 3,100 in 1953 to about 2,758 in 2007, but the number is relatively stable. In those three countries, relatively small size municipalities are generally considered to be preferred, and the scale of the number of the municipalities and the changes in number reflect those preferences.

In contrast, Japan's experience is dramatically different. Japan began modern local governmental administration during the Meiji Restoration of 1868. At that time, more than 70,000 villages existed. The consolidation movement then began, and in the Great Meiji Consolidation the number of villages remarkably decreased to about 15,000. Japan subsequently conducted two more great consolidations, as described in the next section.

Figure 3.4 shows that the changes in basic local governments reflect the social contexts of their countries. It is likely that Japan made great use of its consolidation option to respond to the needs of regional governments. However, at the same time Japan also effectively used the cooperative approach. Even in *San-shinpo* (three new ordinances), which were local administrative legal systems enacted in 1878, the cooperative systems of towns and villages were anticipated. Japan's wide-area administrative methods (wide-area methods) have been ongoing, and there were 7,921 wide-area methods in 2012. Japan is a country that has responded to the needs of a wide-area (regional) agenda by consolidating and cooperating.

Consolidation

This section describes the path of local governmental consolidations in Japan. The consolidations were conducted in the municipalities (basic local governments). These consolidations were initiated by the central government. The basic history follows.

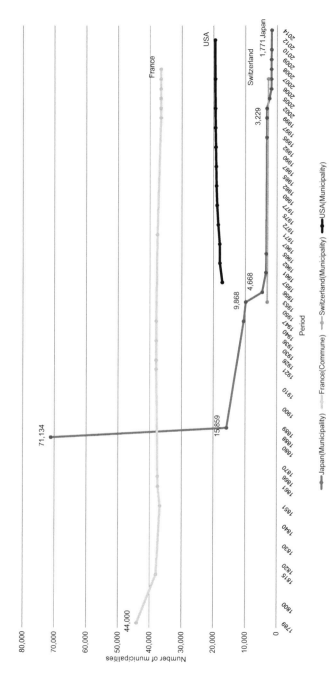

Figure 3.4 Number of basic local governments in France, Switzerland, the US, and Japan from 1789–2014

Source: Created by the author.

Changes in the number of municipalities

Outline

Table 3.1 shows the variation in the numbers of municipalities across time. The number of prefectures has remained the same at 47 since 1888. However, municipalities decreased from 71,314 in 1888 to 1,718 in 2014. The primary reason for this large decrease is the municipal consolidations that particularly occurred during the three great consolidations.

Table 3.1 Changes in the numbers of municipalities across the three great consolidations

	City	Town	Village	Total	Events
1888	–	–	–	71,314	
					Great Meiji Consolidation Standard minimum size *300–500 households*
					• To properly execute such functions as elementary school, taxation, family register, etc.
1889	39	15,820		15,859	Municipal Government Act (1889.4)
1945.10	205	1,797	8,518	10,520	
1947.8	210	1,784	8,511	10,505	Local Autonomy Law (1947.5)
1953.10	286	1,966	7,616	9,868	Towns and Villages Amalgamation Promotion Law (1953.10; expired in 1956.9)
					Great Showa Consolidation Standard minimum size *8,000 in population* • To effectively manage at least one junior high school.
1956.4	495	1,870	2,303	4,668	New Municipality Construction Law (1956.6; expired in 1961.6)
1956.9	498	1,903	1,574	3,975	
1961.6	556	1,935	981	3,472	
1965.4	560	2,005	827	3,392	Law concerning Special Measures for Municipal Amalgamations (1965.3; effective for 10 years)
1995.4	663	1,994	577	3,234	3rd extension of the preceding law (1995.3; expired in 2005.3)
1999.4	671	1,990	568	3,229	Great Heisei Consolidation
2002.4	675	1,981	562	3,218	
2005.3	732	1,423	366	2,521	

(*Continued*)

Table 3.1 (Continued)

	City	Town	Village	Total	Events
2005.4	739	1,317	339	2,395	Law concerning Special Measures, etc. for Municipal Amalgamations (2005.4; will expire in 2010.3) • Reduction of special financial measures (LAT, special loans).
2006.4	779	844	197	1,820	
2007.4	782	827	195	1,804	
2008.4	783	812	193	1,788	
2009.4	783	802	192	1,777	
2010.2	783	799	189	1,771	
2010.4	786	757	184	1,727	
2014.4	790	745	183	1,718	

Source: Created by the author using data from MIC.

The first of these was the Great Meiji Consolidation of 1888–1889, when the number of municipalities declined to about one-fifth of the original size, from 71,314 to 15,859. Between 1953 and 1961, the Great Showa Consolidation was conducted, resulting in a further decrease of about two-thirds, from 9,868 to 3,472. Finally, the Great Heisei Consolidation was implemented between 1999 and 2010, which decreased the number of municipalities by about one-half, from 3,229 to 1,727 (Table 3.1).

Characteristics of the three great consolidations

The Great Meiji Consolidation

When Japan began modernizing after the Meiji Restoration of 1867, numerous local governments were examined. During the ensuing legislative reform of local governments, the Municipal Government Act was implemented (in 1889) as described in Chapter 2. This was a national law for establishing the new governance methods in cities, towns, and villages. Before the Municipal Government Act, the Great Meiji Consolidation was conducted to establish cities, towns, and villages as modern governments.

Until that change, towns and villages were substantially governed like the natural village communities of feudalism that existed between the seventeenth and nineteenth centuries. Most towns and villages that emerged from the changes were derived directly from villages that had originated as joint agricultural production units. They were very small, totaled 48,420, and almost 70% of them had fewer than 100 families in their jurisdictions. They were unable to handle the standards of modern services expected of them. During that period, "the prosperous country and strong army" and "encouragement of new industry" were the slogans and building a modern state was a primary national goal. Therefore, establishing functional local governments was necessary. These governments were expected be functional enough to register families, levy taxes, and operate schools for education that was compulsory at the time. It was obvious that the governments that managed very small jurisdictions would not be able to handle those tasks. Therefore, the notion of allowing small governments to consolidate to form merged local governments was pursued, which was intended to give them greater capacities to function as modern administrative units. The resulting policy was that municipal consolidations were to be accomplished so that units, ranging from "at least 300 to 500 or more households" would be formed. The result was that the number of municipalities decreased from 71,314 in 1888 to 15,859 in 1889.

One step taken by the central government toward achieving consolidations was its decree of June 13, 1888, stating that the central government would not enforce consolidations but would delegate the matter to the prefectures' planning and decisions. However, the central government also decreed that:

(1) the municipalities to which the new laws would apply would (in principle) be existing municipalities,
(2) except in cases of municipalities that were too small, which would be permitted to merge together, and
(3) the standard size of new merged municipalities would range from 300 to 500 households.

Therefore, the initiatives of the governors are believed to have been strong. Moreover, the 71,314 municipalities that existed at the end of 1888 decreased by about four-fifths to about 15,820 in one year's time (by the end of 1889). This significantly large number of mergers in one year strongly suggests that there were promotional intentions among the prefectures in the background, although the municipalities initiated the mergers.

The Great Showa Consolidation

After World War II, the postwar governmental system was established under the new constitution and Local Autonomy Law (LAL), both of which went into effect in 1947. Simultaneously, the Japanese economy failed to start up smoothly, and the domestic stocks of materials were exhausted. Japan's central government and local governments struggled with recovery from the postwar devastation of the 1940s. However, the first half of the 1950s was a time of transition from the period of reconstruction to a period of technological innovation.

In the latter half of the 1950s through the 1960s, the Japanese economy made significant progress. During that time, the structures and functions of municipalities were remarkably increased to give them responsibility for basic local public services, such as the management of junior high schools, fire prevention, and social welfare matters. These public services were believed to be indispensable to the enrichment of civil life.

The Great Showa Consolidation was implemented to create municipalities that could perform these new functions, and management of junior high schools was a particularly essential duty. The municipal consolidations were planned and carried out to create municipalities with populations greater than 8,000 because that was considered to be the minimum size deemed necessary for effectively managing junior high schools.

Similar to the Great Meiji Consolidation, the Great Showa Consolidation was not mandated by the central government. Regarding each municipality's interests, the consolidation was legally determined by the governors of the prefectures based on the relevant municipal assemblies' decisions. However, the national government set forth the Municipality Merger Promotion Master Plan to set the goal of reducing the number of municipalities to one-third its size. Moreover, the central government formally supported the consolidations by collaborating with the prefectures. Therefore, the Great Showa Consolidation is believed to have been conducted in a context of substantial urging by the central government. The number of municipalities decreased from 9,868 in 1953 to 3,975 in 1956, which met the goal of reducing the number of municipalities to one-third.

The Great Heisei Consolidation

The Great Heisei Consolidation began in 1999 and resulted in a decrease in the number of municipalities by about one-half, from 3,229 in 1999 to 1,727 in 2010. The Great Heisei Consolidation was implemented in a unique context. Among other things, it was a necessary response to the ongoing process of decentralization, and the local governments were financially deteriorating. These conditions actually intensified the consolidation's influence on local governments' administrative management. The municipal consolidations were necessary to reinforce their administrative and financial foundations and install more efficient municipal public services.

The first critical factor related to this consolidation was decentralization. With the enactment of the Uniform Decentralization Law in April of 2000, local governments in Japan entered a new stage. The biggest change was the abolition of the delegated function system. In that system, the central government appointed the head of the chief executives of the local governments (governors/mayors) as executive branches of the central government and delegated regulatory power to them. Therefore, abolition of that system was a fundamental reform with respect to the local autonomy of the governmental system.

After that reform, municipalities were expected to conduct all of their administrative business independent of each other under the principle of autonomous decision making.

It was controversial, and in the process the municipalities were strongly encouraged to transition into increased administrative capacities. Some of the municipalities argued that consolidation and increased competencies of local governments were requisite for transferring the numerous administrative duties. In that context, the Great Heisei Consolidation was powerfully advanced (Figure 3.5).

The second critical factor in this consolidation was the need to financially rehabilitate the municipalities. Trends in outstanding local government borrowing have demonstrated about JPY 140 trillion (Figure 3.6).

The payment of local debt was about 13.4% of the total expenditures of the local governments in 2013, and local governments' social assistance

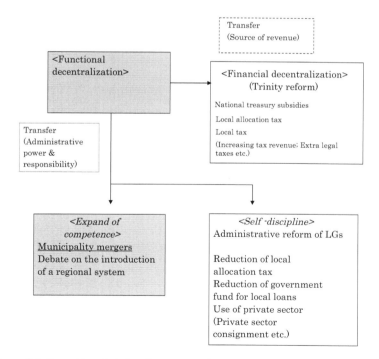

Figure 3.5 Recent trends in local government
Source: Created by the author.

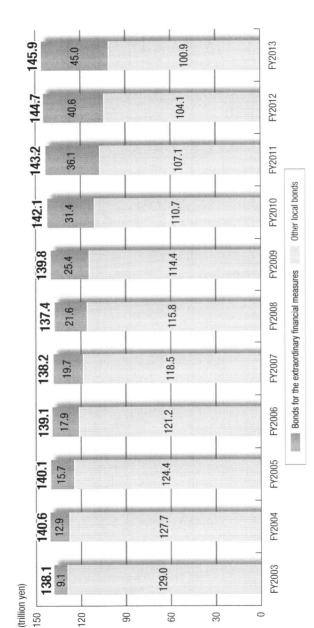

Figure 3.6 Trends in local government borrowing

Source: "White paper on local public finance, 2015 (FY 2013 Settlement)," MIC.

expenses were about 12.5% of total expenditures during the same year, an amount that has been continuously growing (Figure 3.7).

Social assistance expenses comprise elderly welfare services, nursing services, child welfare services, and handicapped services, which are downwardly rigid in their dispositions (Figure 3.8).

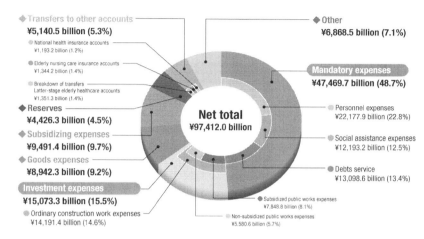

Figure 3.7 Breakdown of local governmental expenditures (FY 2013 Settlement)
Source: "*White paper on local public finance, 2015 (FY 2013 Settlement),*" MIC.

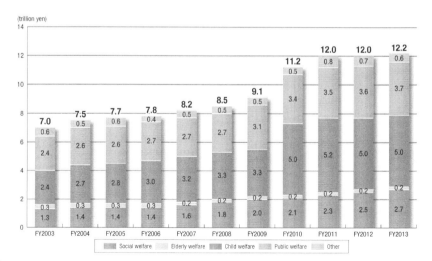

Figure 3.8 Trends in the breakdown of types of social assistance expenses
Source: "*White paper on local public finance, 2015 (FY 2013 Settlement),*" MIC.

The relatively small municipalities have been struggling with these heavy financial burdens. The municipalities were named as the insurers of the nursing insurance system in 2000. As the actual burdens have become clear, the municipalities have become sensitive to the administrative financial burdens. Therefore, among the social factors that determine the size of a local government (Figure 3.1), financial stability is a key element in many local governments' decision-making processes.

In response to these conditions, the Ministry of Internal Affairs and Communications (MIC) formulated the "Guidelines for the Further Promotion of Administrative Reform in Local Governments" on August 31, 2006, which asked local governments to make positive efforts toward three reforms. Under the Guidelines, the local governments moved to act as follows: (1) to reform total personnel expenses, (2) to reform public services, and (3) to reform local public accounting. Among the several methods available to achieve these reforms, consolidation was an effective approach. Thus, the combination of the problems faced locally and the encouragements of the central government functioned to direct local governments toward the option of consolidation (Figure 3.5).

As was true for the two previous consolidations, the Great Heisei Consolidation was not mandatory. However, deteriorating finances and population aging in the local communities tended to push many chief executive officers toward discussions among the municipalities, which occurred throughout the country, yielding many consolidations.

In 2008 MIC conducted a survey in order to look into the advantages and challenges of the Great Heisei Consolidation; Figure 3.9 shows the outcome of that survey. The local governments which experienced the consolidation answered the question: why did they consolidate? The answer with the most responses was to address financial problems, and the third most common response was "to address the aging population." Those answers suggest that the local governments were facing severe financial challenges and growing financial demand for the aging populations (Figure 3.9).

Changes in the compositions of municipalities

A close examination of the results to separately examine cities distinct from towns and villages reveals important information. First, in the Great Meiji Consolidation, the number of towns and villages decreased from 71,314 to 15,820, although 39 new cities were created. Then, in the Great Showa Consolidation, the number of villages was remarkably reduced from 7,616 to 981, and the number of towns was modestly reduced from 1,966 to 1,935. During the same period, the number of cities almost doubled from 286 to 556 (Table 3.1). Third, in the Great Heisei Consolidation, the number of villages

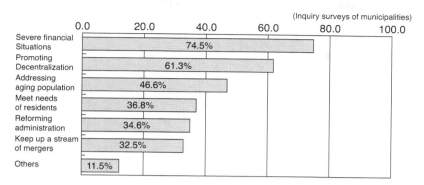

Figure 3.9 Reasons for mergers

Source: Created by the author using "Evaluation, verification and analysis of the Great Heisei Amalgamation," MIC, June 2008. (Multiple answers allowed.)

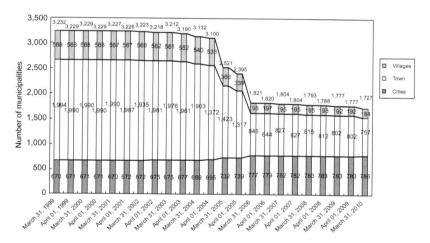

Figure 3.10 Changes in the number of municipalities in the Great Heisei Consolidation
Source: Data from MIC.

markedly decreased from 568 to 198, and the number of towns decreased from 1,990 to 846, but the number of cities increased from 671 to 777 (Table 3.3 and Figure 3.10).

In sum, it is clear that the numbers of villages and towns markedly decreased, whereas the number of cities increased in all three of the great

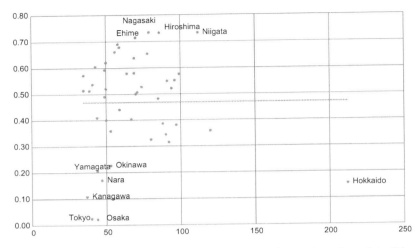

Figure 3.11 Scatter plot of the relationship between the number of municipalities and the ratio of decrease by prefecture

Source: Created by the author.

consolidations. In the context of their financial crises and increasing social services' expenditures, the great consolidation movement greatly reduced the number of small-scale governments.

Next, the discussion of the consolidation is carried out at the municipality level. The related municipalities establish a council which takes council together. The consolidation is not mandated, and the final decision depends on the agreement of the council. In this composition the central government and the prefecture play roles as advisers. However, the prefectures substantially have also played significant roles.

Figure 3.11 shows regional differences that resulted from the Great Heisei Consolidation between 1999 and 2010.

A: Number of municipalities (after consolidation movement, 2006)
B: Number of municipalities (before consolidation movement, 1999)

$$\text{Ratio of decrease} = \frac{B-A}{B} \times 100(\%)$$

In Figure 3.11, the horizontal axis shows the number of municipalities by prefecture in 1999 before the Great Heisei Consolidation. The vertical axis shows the proportional decrease in the number because of the consolidation movement.

The following points are made:

1   There were substantial differences in the proportional decrease among the prefectures. The decrease of the higher rate decreasing group of prefectures (such as Niigata, Hiroshima, and Nagasaki) exceeded 0.7, meaning that the number of municipalities decreased to about one-third of their pre-consolidation number. On the other hand, the lower rate decreasing group of prefectures (such as Tokyo and Osaka) decreased less than 0.1.

2   The correlation between the number of municipalities and the proportional decrease is very weak ($r = .0015$). This finding indicates that the prefectures with many municipalities did not necessarily achieve a significant number of consolidations.

Actually some prefectures were famous for aggressively giving boosts to the consolidations in their districts. These data back up the relation of the approaches and the results. The data suggests that the extent of a prefecture's aggressiveness as an advisor was expected to have a positive effect on the number of consolidations.

Figure 3.12 shows Hyogo prefecture. In 1999, before the Great Heisei Consolidation it had 91 municipalities; this number decreased to 41 by 2010. Some neighboring municipalities advanced in the consolidation, as shown in Figure 3.12.

Because of the three great consolidations, the average population size of basic local governments grew to 73,000 in Japan (see Table 3.6). Except for the UK, which established large governmental jurisdictions through local administrative reforms, the average sizes in some other countries are much smaller than in Japan. For example, the average size in the US is 16,000; in France, it is less than 2,000; in Germany and Italy, it is less than 7,000. Thus, the sizes of the basic local governments in Japan are relatively large as a result of the consolidations. Those consolidations also brought numerous other changes to Japan's communities, but Japan should continue to advance toward a new stage of even larger basic local governments.

Cooperation

Figure 3.3 shows that responding to the needs of the regional citizenry, local governments have two options. One is to consolidate and the other is to cooperate. As explained in the previous section, Japan has progressed regarding consolidations. However, Japan also has effectively used cooperation. The cooperative systems are the wide-area administrative methods as stipulated in the LAL. In this section, we focus on cooperation.

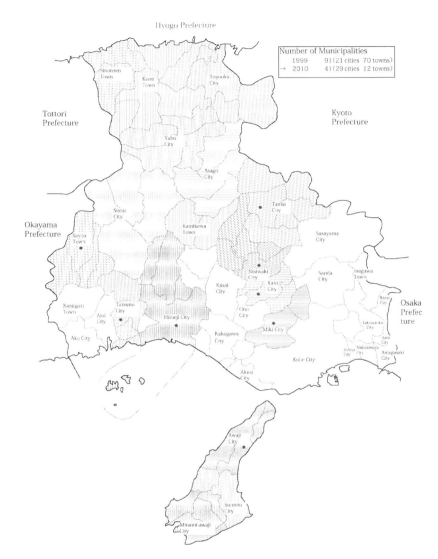

Figure 3.12 Hyogo prefecture
Source: Created by the author using Google Maps.

Regional needs have encouraged the development of cooperative arrangements to the present. This is a globally common development: Japan and other Western countries have pursued wide-area cooperation (Chapter 2, Table 2.6). For example, as shown in the bottom row of Table 2.6, the US has special districts, school districts, and so on; the UK has combined authorities, joint boards, and so on; France has SIVU, Métropole, and so on; Germany has Ober Regionale-gemeindeverland, Amt/Samt Gemeinde, and so on; and Italy has Unione di comuni, Comunità montane, and so on.

History of wide-area government

Under the Imperial Constitution (before the end of World War II)

The original form of wide-area government was founded before World War II under the Imperial Constitution. In the 1870s, the unions of towns/ villages were established as a general practice. *San-shinpo* (three new ordinances) was enacted in 1878 to provide the union of several towns/ villages. The *Chosonsei* (town/village act) was enacted in 1888 to provide for the unions of towns and villages. This was the first regional cooperation legal system in Japan. Subsequently, the amendment of the *Shisei* (city act) in 1891 provided for the unions of municipalities, and the amendment of the *Fukensei* (prefecture act) in 1914 provided for the unions of prefectures.

The context in which the governmental system existed in the Imperial Constitution period is as follows:

1   Even in the formative period of Japan's local governmental system, there were some administrative demands that municipalities, as general governments, could not meet, and a regional administrative approach, such as the unions of towns and villages, was required.
2   In the 1880s, there were more than 71,000 municipalities. Supporting and supplementing the capacities of the relatively small towns and villages was a pressing issue.
3   In the late nineteenth century, the consolidation of municipalities was an urgent matter in Japan. When consolidation was difficult because of geographic or other conditions, the unions of towns and villages were the alternative approach.

The social context in the nineteenth century was different from the current one, but the idea of the unions as alternatives to ordinary governments popular at that time would be applicable today.

The new constitution (post–World War II)

Under the new constitution of 1947, LAL provided the basic structure of the local governmental system. The constitution and the LAL inherited the union system for wide-area cooperative methods. In addition, a major devolution to municipalities was conducted in the postwar institutional reforms. For example, the municipalities took on the responsibility of operating the new compulsory education.

However, because individual ordinary governments found it difficult to fully respond to their increasing administrative demands, the promotion of wide-area administrations was planned by the central government. In the 1952 amendment to the LAL, the councils, the shared administrative organizations, and the delegation of duties were provided for reducing the expenses and improving the efficiency of administrations. The 1952 amendment was the substantial starting point of full-scale wide-area administration in the Japanese local governmental system. Subsequently, in the 1956 amendment to the LAL, a system for managing personnel was introduced to improve efficiency.

At the end of the 1960s, as economic growth stabilized, wide-area government in the form of RAZ (the regional administrative zone) was promoted within regional development policies and became a crucial challenge. This idea was not merely about sharing administrative duties across jurisdictions; it was also about developing a vital region through a comprehensive plan and wide-area public services. The Ministry of Home Affairs (now the MIC) issued the "Guidelines for Measures to Promote Regional Municipal Zones in Fiscal 1969." These guidelines stipulated that the municipalities within an RMZ)[2] form a PAA or a council as the regional administrator.[3]

In the 1994 amendment to the LAL, the regional union system was established as the best approach for delegating responsibilities that were deemed to be more appropriately managed regionally than locally. The LAL provided for regional unions as a new type of union, which was a wide-area administrative method with corporate legal status similar to a PAA (as described later). It was anticipated that the Great Heisei Consolidation would decrease the 3,232 municipalities recorded in March 1999 to 1,757 in March 2010 through the consolidations. This local reorganization exerted a significant influence on the methods of forming RAZ that were in place at the time. The number of RAZ formed into one municipality as the result of the Great Heisei Consolidation was 37. RAZ was a policy through the inter-municipal cooperation. When the affiliated local governments of a RAZ became one municipality, the time had come to review the policy.

Under these conditions, in 2008, before the Great Heisei Consolidation concluded, the MIC issued "Guidelines for the Promotion of the Concept of Autonomous Settlement Zones." At the same time, the "Guidelines for the Planning of Wide-area Government Zones of 2000" were abolished.

Around that time the idea of autonomous settlement zones (ASZ) was promoted to stem the emigration of people from rural areas and create a flow of people moving in the opposite direction back into the rural areas. ASZ was formed because of an accumulation of one-to-one agreements concluded on their own initiative between the central city and their surrounding municipalities (see Chapter 4).

Next, the functions of the central cities are emphasized. The process begins with a central city declaration that states its intention to assume a central role in guaranteeing the basic living necessities for the zone as a whole. Next, the central city enters into an agreement to form an autonomous settlement zone; the agreements are specific one-to-one contracts with the surrounding municipalities. This act marks the establishment of an ASZ. The next step is to determine a vision for coexistence for the future of the ASZ; the vision includes the actual activities based on the agreement for forming an ASZ. It also includes a vision for the future of the zone. As of October 2015, 123 cities had issued central city declarations, there were 95 ASZ, and 92 zones had created their visions for coexistence.

In the 2014 amendment of the LAL, the coalition agreement system was introduced to provide a simple and quick legal method for municipalities to enter into one-to-one agreements. Through these methods, agile management of wide-area governments is expected and attention will be focused on them next.

Types of wide-area government

Outline

Because administrative demands are highly diverse, local governments must be highly specialized and integrated into a broader region, and the number of sectors, whose concerns are believed to be more efficiently and rationally administered under mutual and joint cooperative agreements between or among local governments rather than by individual local governments, is increasing. In this context, a system of joint government of affairs has been adopted. Altogether, there are six types of wide-area methods, and they can be broadly categorized according to whether they have corporate legal status.

Figure 3.13 Methods of wide-area governmental administration
Source: Created by the author.

Considering first those administrators or governments that do require corporate legal status, there are two types: partial-affairs associations (PAAs) and wide-area unions. Both types are referred to as "unions," and they are designated as "special local public entities" under the LAL. In addition, there are four simpler types of systems without corporate legal status: (1) councils, (2) joint establishment of organs and staff, (3) delegation of duties, and (4) dispatch of personnel (Figure 3.13).

Individual method

The scheme of each wide-area method is described in Table 3.2.

Table 3.2 Descriptions of the corporate and non-corporate wide-area methods

Method		Contents of system
Corporate legal status type	Partial-affairs association	The association is established among prefectures, municipalities, or special wards for the purpose of jointly administering a part of their functions. It has a corporate legal status. It is stipulated as a type of union by LAL (see Chapter 2).
	Wide-area union	The union is established by prefectures, municipalities, or special wards in order to make and put into execution comprehensive plans covering a wide geographical area. It has a corporate legal status. It is stipulated as a type of union by LAL (see Chapter 2).
Non-corporate legal status type	Council	An ordinary local public entity may establish a council through which it can consult with other entities to establish regulations and administer a portion of the affairs jointly pursuant to such regulations.
	Shared administrative organization	An ordinary local public entity may consult with other entities to establish regulations and jointly set up committees, affiliated organizations, and executive, and may jointly provide members supplementary personnel and expert members for such committees and organizations pursuant to such regulations.
	Delegation of duties	An ordinary local public entity may consult with other entities to establish regulations and delegate a portion of its affairs to other ordinary local public entities. It may also force the chief executive and committees in similar ordinary local public entities concerned to administer and execute affairs in that portion pursuant to such regulations.
	Dispatch of personnel	A chief executive, committees and the members of a local public entity may request other local public entities to send one or more of their personnel to administer and execute affairs.

Source: Created by the author.

Characteristics of wide-area government

Wide-area methods

THE CURRENT SITUATION

The current legal framework of wide-area government was presented in the LAL in the 1950s (see Chapter 3). Since then, local governments have actively practiced wide-area administrative methods. Table 3.3 shows

Table 3.3 Characteristics of types of wide-area methods (July 1, 2012)

Classification of Wide-Area Local Public Service System (as of July 1,2012, unit: number of cases)

Type of constituent local government	Inter-prefecture (A)	Region composed of several prefectures		In the area of single prefecture		Cooperation between prefectures and municipalities (B) + (D)	Cooperation between municipalities (C) + (E)	Total (A) + (B) + (C) + (D) + (E)	Previous survey (as of July 1,2010)	Increase or decrease
		Cooperation between prefectures and municipalities (B)	Cooperation between municipalities (C)	Cooperation between prefectures and municipalities (D)	Cooperation between municipalities (E)					
Council	1	4	2	7	177	11	179	191	216	−25
Shared administrative organization	–	–	1	1	398	1	399	400	395	5
Delegation of duties	23	56	825	1,693	3,071	1,749	3,896	5,668	5,264	404
Partial-affairs association	2	–	16	37	1,491	37	1,507	1,546	1,572	−26
Regional union	–	1	–	5	109	6	109	115	115	–
Local development association	–	–	–	1	–	1	–	1	1	–
Total	26	61	844	1,744	5,246	1,805	6,090	7,921	7,563	358
Share (%)	0.3	0.8	10.7	22.0	66.2	22.8	76.9	100.0	–	–

Source: "Survey of the system of joint administration in 2014" (MIC).

the status of the establishment of wide-area government as of 2012, as follows.

1   The total number of all types of wide-area methods in 2012 was 7,921, which is a 4.7% increase from 2010 (see also Figure 3.14).
2   The share of cooperative administrations in single prefectures is high: 89.1% (6,990 divided by the total of 7,921).
3   The share of cooperative administrations between municipalities is high: 76.9% (6,090 divided by the total of 7,921).
4   The share of cooperative administrations between prefectures and municipalities was 22.8%. Among them, the delegation of duties type

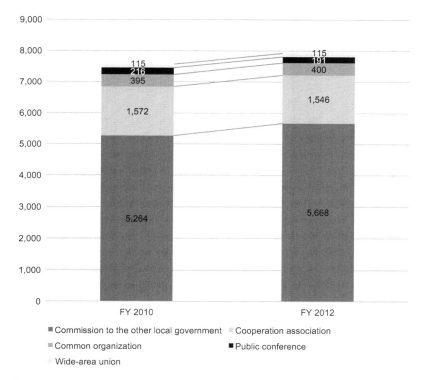

Figure 3.14 Changes to proportional distribution of the types of wide-area methods (July 1, 2012)

Source: Created by the author using "*Survey of the system of joint administration in 2014.*"

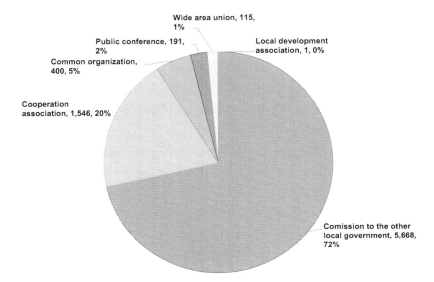

Figure 3.15 Proportional distribution of types of wide-area methods

Source: Created by the author using "*Survey of the system of joint administration in 2014.*"

accounts for 96.9%. The matters that infrequently arise, but never fail to occur, such as equity commissions and compensation for personal accidents in the line of duty, are actively handled by delegation.

5   Considering all the types of methods, the delegation of duties type (71.6%) and the partial-affairs association type (19.5%) account for the largest proportions (Figure 3.15).

THE TREND

Figure 3.16 shows the changes in the types of wide-area methods from 2006 to 2012.

The total number remained essentially the same between 2006 and 2010, but it significantly increased in 2012, mainly because the number of delegation of duties type increased (regarding duties such as issuing residency cards and matters regarding medical care for the advanced elderly) by many administrations.

The number of PAAs continuously decreased, mostly because of the Great Heisei Consolidation. This trend reflects the disbanding of related

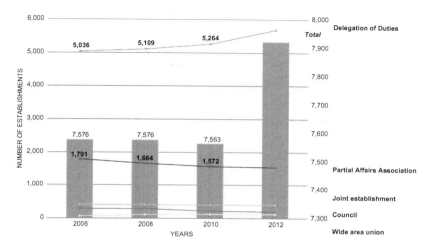

Figure 3.16 Changes in the types of wide-area methods between 2006 and 2012

Source: Created by the author using "*Survey of the system of joint administration in 2014.*"

associations that accompanied less need to merge as the municipalities consolidated.

The numbers of the councils and the shared administrative organizations were mostly stable. Regional unions were quite recently established (in 1996) and their numbers have gradually increased.

Figure 3.4 shows the comparison of the situation in 2010 to that of 2012, in which the increases in the delegation of duties type and the decreases in the partial-affairs association type are obvious.

Partial-affairs association (PAA)

Among the wide-area methods, PAAs have played a major role. Therefore, this section focuses on the structure, status, and agenda of the PAA.

The need for PAA

As explained in Chapter 2 (see Figure 2.2), some local public matters are difficult for individual governments to manage, particularly those that are costly or require significant or specialized staff. For those matters, PAAs have effectively supported and supplemented local governments.

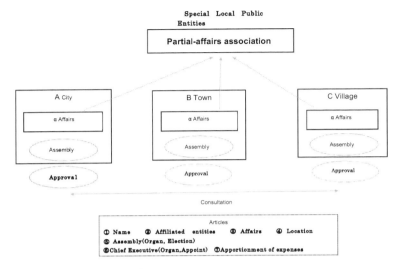

Figure 3.17 The structure of a PAA

Source: Created by the author.

An image of the PAA structure is shown in Figure 3.17.

If a city (A), a town (B), and a village (C) have common concerns (α affairs in Figure 3.17), and they all agree that establishing a PAA would be a reasonable approach to managing those concerns, they can create a PAA and transfer the α affairs to it for administration using the process stipulated by Article 284 of the LAL. The basic characteristics, processes, and responsibilities of PAAs are stipulated by statute. Seven articles cover these basics, as indicated in Figure 3.17.

Merits of PAA

The merits of PAAs for the wide-area method are summarized in Table 3.4.

First, PAAs have corporate legal status, meaning that they can provide public services through large public facilities and therefore cover a wide range of public services. PAAs can manage public services using the Internet and those that require facilities. Second, PAAs use a dual representative system comprising a chief executive, administrator, and deliberative body (PAA assembly). Moreover, the system is based on the principle of checks and balances. This system recognizes the delegation of responsibilities and contributes to the transparency and democratic management of the

Table 3.4 Description of the merits of PAA

Points	Remarks
Corporate legal status	PAAs have the corporate legal status and they can independently carry out the acts of law and can hold properties. Therefore they can supply the public services through the operation of the large public facilities; e.g., refuse disposal, firefighting, nursing home, school house, water supply, hospital.
Dual representative system	PAAs have their own chief executive organizations, assemblies, and auditors. Through those dual representative system (presidential system), they can clarify where the responsibilities lie for their managements.
Disposal of multiple affairs	PAAs can discharge the multiple responsibilities if they define them in their statutes. Moreover the complex-PAA system was established incrementally in 1974; that the affairs were common to all the affiliated governments is not required for the complex-PAA.
Grand-scale budget use	PAAs compile their own budgets. They can make a grand-scale of expenditures through using shares from affiliated governments, local bonds, and so on.

Source: Created by the author.

PAA. Third, PAAs can handle the numerous matters that need to be administered when these matters have been defined in their articles. Moreover, the complex PAA system was incrementally established in 1974; it was not necessary that the services were common to all of the affiliated municipalities. Therefore, it was easier to join a PAA as an affiliate because the PAAs were internally individualized. Fourth, PAAs have independent budgets and they can manage high expenditure by selling shares, local bonds, and so on. Taken together, the merits of a PAA can create comprehensive and stable public administrations. These merits clearly distinguish PAAs from the other types of administration and their superiority has led many local governments to affiliate with PAAs.

Status of the PAA

Constitutional status

PAA is a type of special local administrative system provisioned by the LAL (Article 1.3). Is the PAA system constitutional? Is the PAA system equivalent to the status of local governments as guaranteed by the constitution?

Regarding these questions, it is notable that by judicial precedent, the special district (also a category of special local administrations) is not considered equivalent to local governments as guaranteed by the constitution.

The Supreme court ruled that local governments should be designated as such by national law, according to social conditions, such as community spirit in economically and culturally tight-knit communal lifestyles, and the governance should be a regional institution with basic local autonomous power.[4] In this context, it is reasonable that only the ordinary local governments (municipalities) have the status and rights of local government as guaranteed by the constitution its rules. Consequently, a special local administration's status is provided by national law (the LAL), and the rules applied to PAAs are basically pursuant to the LAL rules that apply to ordinary governments.

However, there are exceptions because some of the LAL's rules that do not fit the characteristics of the PAA are not applied to them. In those cases, the rules established by the PAA regulate it (in those cases, the PAA self-regulates). For example, LAL rules are not applied with respect to the methods of electing the individual administrator or the PAA assembly members, as ruled in the aforementioned court case. A PAA is not given constitutional status, and therefore the PAA members are not considered citizens, but are affiliated local governments (affiliates), as described later. Therefore, the administrator and the assembly members of PAAs are not required to be elected through the direct election. So in many PAAs, the administrators are elected through the mutual election among the heads of the affiliated local governments.

Three elements as local government

The theory of the administrative law lists three elements required for a local government as stated in Chapter 2: area, membership, and functions. How should we understand those three elements with respect to PAAs?

AREA

Local administrations are created based on geographic space in the national territory. Defining the specific area is indispensable for local administrations, which is very different from other types of government. Local administrations can exercise authority inside their bounds. The specified area of a PAA equals the sum of all the areas of all their affiliates. Therefore, the specified area of a PAA can change for several reasons, such as (1) an increase or decrease in the number of affiliates; (2) abolishment, division, or consolidation of their affiliates; or (3) changes to the affiliates' municipal boundaries.

MEMBERSHIP

The overarching objective of local administrations is the improvement of the welfare of the affiliated citizens, and the constituency of the local administration is nothing else but the citizens. Based on this idea, the membership of an ordinary government is considered membership of the citizens. However, a current popular theory argues that in judicial logic the affiliates (local governments) are the direct members and the citizens comprise the indirect membership.

Using this idea, direct suffrage for administrators and PAA assembly members has not been envisaged, and direct elections considered possible only when a PAA's rules provide for them, although no cases of this exist thus far. Along these lines, direct suffrage for the inter-municipal cooperation in France (EPCI) was debated and introduced by the act of modernization of local government and establishment of the French métropolitaine. In the French case, EPCIs have the basic authority of taxation. Therefore, from the perspective of the relationship between democracy and taxation, the suffrage system has been an important issue. On the other hand, in the case of Japan, the special governments are not given any power to tax and, therefore, this issue has not emerged. However, direct elections may become an issue if residential participation intensifies in the future.

FUNCTIONS

The local government's basic function is to control public administration in its geographic area for the public benefit of its residents. Upon joining a PAA, an affiliate transfers its functions as the ordinary government to the PAA. However, the PAA is limited to the determinate function as a wide-area administrative method among the affiliates. Such confirmed function is stipulated by the statutes of the PAA. Within the realm of that function, the PAA can enact bylaws and rules, secure sources of revenue, and exercise public authority. Moreover, it is important to note that PAAs have no rights of taxation in Japan's local governmental system.[5] These distinctions have influenced PAAs financing capacities and led to financial dependency on the affiliates' funds.

Legal framework of PAA

The basic legal structure of PAAs is stipulated by Article 284 of the LAL as follows. The local governments can establish a PAA to jointly administer some of their services or other matters by means of these processes stipulated by the LAL.

> **Article 284** Unions of local public bodies shall be classified into partial unions and wide-area unions.
>
> **2.** Local public bodies or special wards may agree by consultation and with the approval of the Minister of Internal Affairs and Communications in the case of a To, Do, Fu or Ken or of the governor of the To, Do, Fu or Ken in the case of other local public bodies, to establish a partial union of local public bodies for the purpose of managing jointly a part of the affairs of the local public bodies.

Affairs of PAA

PAAs are not regulated to the extent they are in the jurisdictions of the local governments that are their affiliates. When the several local governments agree to jointly administer some of their services or other matters and establish a PAA, they can simply give all responsibility for those matters to the PAA.

The types of matters that can be administered by a PAA are shown in Figure 3.6. The asset in production type is when the affiliates provide public services through making use of facilities ranks proportionally high. The services are environmental sanitation, disaster prevention, public welfare (Figure 3.18), and so on.

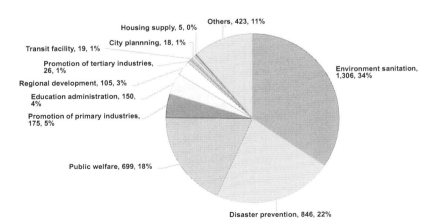

Figure 3.18 Types of services and other matters administered by PAAs as of 2012
Source: Created by the author using "Survey of the system of joint administration in 2014."

A PAA has corporate legal status as shown in Table 3.4. Therefore, a PAA independently contracts with and holds the asset of its own and it can manage its responsibilities with large budgets. This is why a PAA is suitable for this type of administration (Figure 3.18).

Trends of the PAA

The number of PAAs has continuously declined since its peak in 1972 (Figure 3.19). This was mostly caused by the Great Heisei Consolidation, as explained earlier in this chapter). Because the affiliates merged, there were no need in some cases to retain the related PAAs; when the affiliates consolidated, the city that resulted from that consolidation was often likely to be able to administer successfully.

It is important to note that the number of PAAs particularly decreased from 1,572 in 2010 to 1,546 in 2012 (Figure 3.19). However, the number of services and other matters covered by PAAs increased during that time, from 3,779 in 2010 to 3,791 in 2012 (Table 3.5 and Figure 3.20).

This happened because the existing PAAs added services. When we consider the disaggregated data, public welfare services (plus 8), disaster prevention (plus 7), and environment sanitation services (plus 4) all increased. Those services are so crucial to municipal administration that municipalities are believed to pursue the more effective public services through PAA membership.

Making use of the wide-area administrative methods shown in Figure 3.13 is discretionary in principle. Whether the method is adopted among the affiliates depends on the agreements among them. Then where are the wide-area administrative methods aggressively used? Are many methods adopted in a region where a lot of municipalities are located?

Figure 3.21 shows the relationship of the number of municipalities per prefecture to the number of communal disposals per prefecture.

The correlation is weak ($r = .489$), suggesting that regions with many municipalities do not always set up many communal disposals. The alternative causes, such as the developments and motivations of the local governments, may influence the observed differences among the prefectures. However, each local government should explore their options for additional effective utilization for the wide-area administrative methods.

Next, Figure 3.22 shows the relationship between the number of municipalities per prefecture and the number of PAAs per prefecture.

The correlation is quite strong ($r = .821$), suggesting that PAAs have been such a principal method among the types of the wide-area administrative methods that PAAs became positively established in regions with many municipalities.

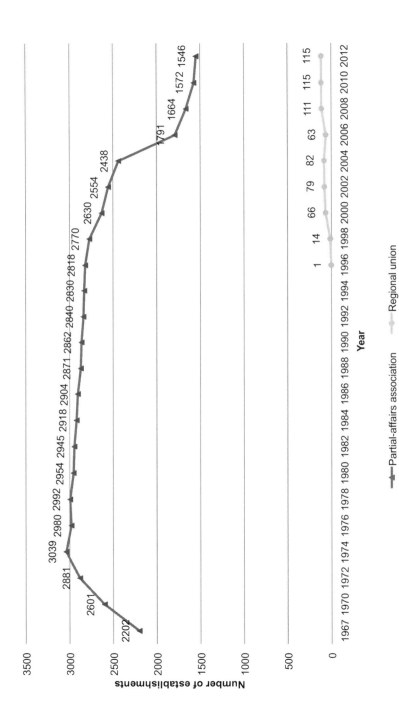

Figure 3.19 Changes of numbers of PAAs and regional unions

Source: Created by the author using "Survey of the system of joint administration in 2014."

Table 3.5 Types and numbers of services and other matters covered by PAA (FY 2010 and FY 2012)

	Assortment of cooperative processing	Affairs covered by PAA		
		FY 2010	FY 2012	Increase/ decrease
1 Regional development		142	105	−37
2 Promotion of primary industries		174	175	1
3 Promotion of secondary industries		14	16	2
4 Promotion of tertiary industries		27	26	−1
5 Transit facility		20	19	−1
6 Country maintenance		3	3	—
7 Public welfare		691	699	8
8 Environment sanitation		1,302	1,306	4
9 Education administration		154	150	−4
10 Housing supply		5	5	—
11 City planning		16	18	2
12 Disaster prevention		839	846	7
13 Others (Fire defence and such)		392	423	31
Total		3,779	3,791	12

Source: Created by the author using *"Survey of the system of joint administration in 2014."*

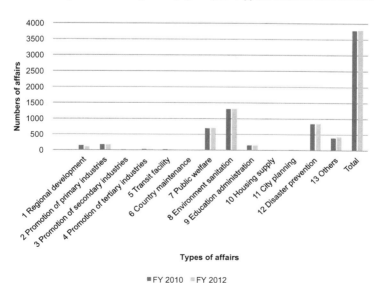

Figure 3.20 Changes in the types of services administered by PAAs (2010 and 2012)
Source: Created by the author using *"Survey of the system of joint administration in 2014."*

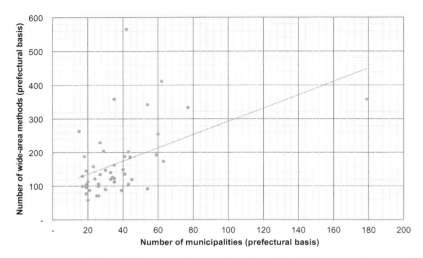

Figure 3.21 Relationship between the number of municipalities per prefecture and the number of wide-area administrative methods by prefecture

Source: Created by the author using "*Survey of the system of joint administration in 2014.*"

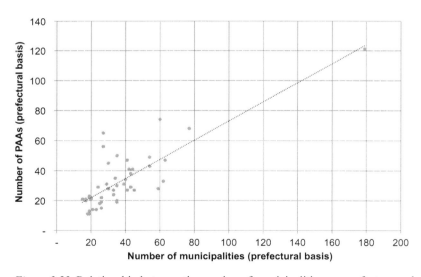

Figure 3.22 Relationship between the number of municipalities per prefecture and the number of PAAs per prefecture

Source: Created by the author using "*Survey of the system of joint administration in 2014.*"

Establishment of PAA

Adequacy

An examination of the status of PAAs reveals some issues.

Case A: Among the affiliates, one affiliate (the central city) bears a relatively heavier financial burden and that affiliate substantially assumes the responsibilities of its neighboring affiliates.

Case B: The primary objective for establishing a PAA is to disperse the responsibilities for nuisance services, such as garbage disposal, and the financial burdens. Moreover, the affiliates have little interest in the effective management of the PAA.

What causes these problems? They are caused by the imperfect consensus for the strategic management of the PAA. How to effectively and efficiently operate the PAA is a key issue when the affiliates decide to establish the PAA. Therefore checking against the adequacy for establishment of new PAA is requisite before the affiliates make a political response for establishing the PAA, as the wide-area administrative organization. Figure 3.23 shows those checking processes.

When the affiliates consider a PAA before joining it, they should carefully examine the necessity, efficiency, assuredness, and democratic features of the PAA. The concrete questions to be addressed are shown in Figure 3.23.

Organization

The process by which a PAA should be organized is stipulated in Article 284 of the LAL.

First, de facto consultations among the potential affiliates are held, in which they consider the contents of statutes, such as the organizational design that includes the structure of the chief executive officer of the PAA, the structure of the assembly members, methods of election, matters and services to be administered by the PAA, the burden of charges to the affiliates, and so on.

Second, each mayor (chief executive officer) of the potential affiliates submits a bill of incorporation of the PAA and a bill of the draft of the statute. Third, after each individual assembly approves the bills, the chief executive officers of the potential affiliates conduct an official consultation. If all the potential affiliates are municipalities, the chief executive officers submit the application to organize the PAA to the governor (of the prefecture). Otherwise, they submit the application to the minister of MIC (Figure 3.24).

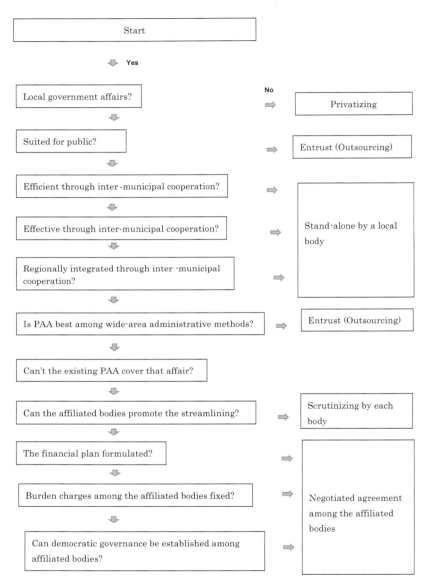

Start

Yes

Local government affairs? → No → Privatizing

Suited for public? → Entrust (Outsourcing)

Efficient through inter-municipal cooperation? →

Effective through inter-municipal cooperation? → Stand-alone by a local body

Regionally integrated through inter-municipal cooperation? →

Is PAA best among wide-area administrative methods? → Entrust (Outsourcing)

Can't the existing PAA cover that affair?

Can the affiliated bodies promote the streamlining? → Scrutinizing by each body

The financial plan formulated? →

Burden charges among the affiliated bodies fixed? → Negotiated agreement among the affiliated bodies

Can democratic governance be established among affiliated bodies? →

Figure 3.23 Checking flow for establishing a PAA

Source: Created by the author using "Survey of the system of joint administration in 2014."

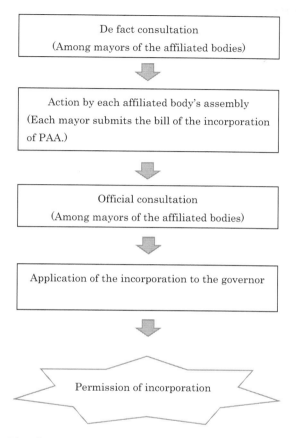

Figure 3.24 Flow for establishing a PAA when all the potential affiliates are municipalities

Source: Created by the author using "Survey of the system of joint administration in 2014."

Structure of PAA

A PAA is established through consultation among the affiliates (Article 284 of
the LAL). This consultation among the potential affiliates is a joint legal act.[6]

A PAA is a special local administration and the LAL is applied accordingly (Article 292, LAL). Therefore, the structure of a PAA is pursuant to
the ordinary government.

The structure is based on the dual representative system. Therefore, a
PAA is planned as the dual representative system similar to the ordinary
governments. An image of the structure of a PAA is shown in Figure 3.25.

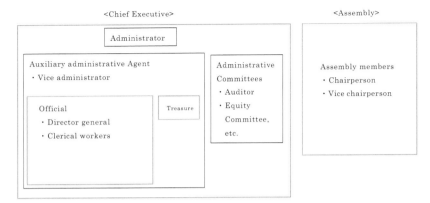

Figure 3.25 Structure of PAAs

Source: Created by the author using "*Survey of the system of joint administration in 2014.*"

A PAA's chief executive officer and assembly are expected to manage the services and other matters through the system of checks and balances as shown in Figure 2.11.

The head of the PAA is called the administrator. The administrator has the status and functions similar to a governor or mayor of an ordinary local government pursuant to the LAL. The administrator has the administrative responsibilities, including submitting bills to the assembly. The PAA assembly has the function of making resolutions, submitting bills, investigating duties, and so on.

Both the administrator and the assembly use their initiative methods and, through checks and balances, the administrative affairs are conducted (see Chapter 2).

Application of the LAL to PAA

The LAL stipulates the Application of LAL Provisions for Ordinary Local Public Bodies to PAA as follows:

Article 292.
Except as otherwise provided by laws or cabinet orders duly authorized by laws, provisions on To, Do, Fu or Ken shall apply mutatis mutandis to unions of local public bodies comprising To, Do, Fu or Ken; provisions on cities shall apply mutatis mutandis to those composing cities and special wards but not To, Do, Fu, or Ken; and provisions on towns or villages shall apply mutatis mutandis to the other unions.

The PAA is the special government and it has a lot in common with the ordinary government. Therefore it is thought to be reasonable to apply the LAL mutatis mutandis to the special government.

Statutes of PAA

The LAL is mutatis mutandis applied to PAA as the basic management rule, but some items are exclusively set down by a PAA's statute. Statutes provide the fundamental structure and rules of a PAA; those are basic rules that govern PAAs. When the affiliates agree about the establishment of a PAA, they arrive at the agreement on the contents of the statute of the PAA at the same time.

Article 287.
A partial union shall provide for the following matters in its agreement.

1 The name of the partial union;
2 The local public bodies composing the partial union;
3 The affairs to be managed jointly by the partial union;
4 The place of the office of the partial union;
5 The composition of the assembly of the partial union and the manner of election of its members;
6 The composition of the chief executive officers of the partial union and the manner of appointment;
7 The manner of apportionment of the expenses of the partial union.

The consultation substantially has the capacity to enact law and the statutes are the subsisting basis of PAA and are binding on the affiliates. Therefore, the bylaws and rules enacted by the PAA should be compatible with the statutes regarding it. There are seven necessary articles (Article 287 of the LAL) (Figure 3.26).

Items of Statutes
1 Name 2 Affiliates 3 Affairs 4 Place of Office
5 Assembly (Composition, Election)
6 Chief Executive Officers (Composition, Appointment)
7 Apportionment of expenses

Figure 3.26 Required items of PAA statutes
Source: Created by the author.

If any one of them is missing, the statute is invalid, and establishment is not approved by minister or governor. The reasons for requiring these items are as follows.

Name

There is no specific legal regulation regarding the name of a PAA. However, a PAA is expected to pay attention to following points.

1　The name should include the "partial-affairs association."
2　The name should also include the types of matters that association administers, such as fire defense or public affairs association.
3　The name can include the name of the *gun* (county) if the affiliates are all the members of that county to clarify the PAA's identity.

Affiliates

Each affiliate should be named in the statutes. If all of the affiliates are municipalities of a prefecture, a description, such as "all the municipalities of X prefecture" is considered acceptable. However, if the number of affiliates is about 10 (e.g., all of the municipalities of a county), listing each one would be appropriate.

Affairs (services and other matters)

The function of a PAA is valid within the scope of the named services and matters of communal disposal, and the affiliates forfeit responsibility for that function at the same time the PAA assumes it. For example, if Town X establishes a PAA regarding fire defense with Village Y, X and Y lose the individual authority to enact fire prevention bylaws. The matters of the communal disposal should be written in the statutes as specifically as possible.

Place of office

Place of office means the location of the main office. The block number should be specified in the statutes. A PAA must observe Article 4(2) of the LAL. In establishing or moving the office location in accord with the preceding paragraph, consideration must be given to the traffic conditions, geographic proximity to other public offices, and so on to maximize the convenience of the residents.

Assembly

Assembly seats, terms, chairpersons, vice chairpersons, methods of election, and panels of candidates should be stipulated in the statutes. The method of

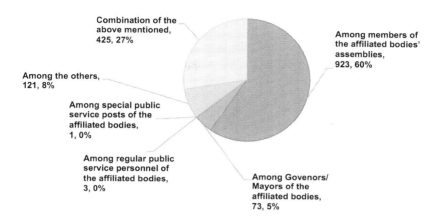

Figure 3.27 Parent populations of PAA assembly members, 2012

Source: Created by the author using "*Survey of the system of joint administration in 2014.*"

electing PAA assembly members is the "term of statutes." The statutes of the PAA specifically describe the method. The ordinary local governments that are affiliates must use direct suffrage, which is very different from the rule in ordinary local governments. Statutes set forth the number of assembly members, the parent population of the elected PAA assembly, and the election methods. Figure 3.27 shows the parent populations of the PAA assemblies in 2012.

PAA assembly members elected from the members of the affiliates' assemblies amount to 923, which was proportionally the largest type of parent population. There were 73 assembly members elected from among governors or mayors, and 121 members were elected from among the public service personnel. This shows that the PAA assembly is closely connected to the affiliates' assemblies and, therefore, the affiliates' assemblies comprise the largest parent population. Figure 3.28 shows the variation in methods of election in 2012.

Voting in the affiliates' assemblies means that each assembly selects its representatives through the election among its assembly members. This way was used by 874, which was the highest proportion. Mutual election means that governors/mayors assume the posts. In this case governors/mayors of the affiliated bodies select PAA assembly members through mutual election. This way was used by 146, which was the second highest proportion. Concurrent post, which refers to the way certain post members (affiliated body's assembly members, governors/mayors and such) automatically accedes to the PAA assembly, was used by 67, the third highest proportion. The election method depends on the statutes, and the actual method used varied in 2012; but, voting in the affiliates' assemblies was the most popular method. This method is equivalent to indirect election by residents.

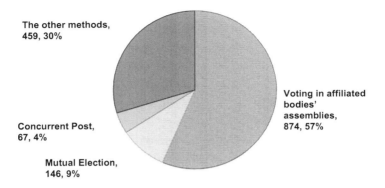

Figure 3.28 Methods of election to PAA assemblies, 2012

Source: Created by the author using *"Survey of the system of joint administration in 2014."*

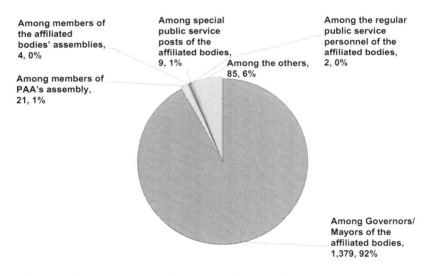

Figure 3.29 The parent populations of PAA administrators

Source: Created by the author using *"Survey of the system of joint administration in 2014."*

Chief executive officers

The role of the chief executive officer and the method of appointment of the administrator are determined by statutes (Article 287 of the LAL). Figure 3.29 shows the parent populations of the PAA administrators.

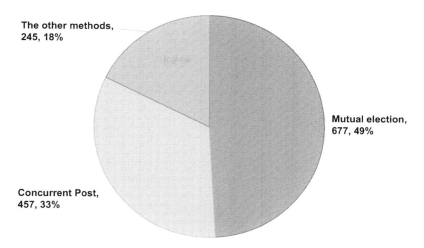

The other methods, 245, 18%

Mutual election, 677, 49%

Concurrent Post, 457, 33%

Figure 3.30 Methods of appointment

Source: Created by the author using "*Survey of the system of joint administration in 2014.*"

There were 1,379 (91.9%) administrators elected from among governors or mayors. Only 21 were elected from among members of the PAAs' assemblies. Most PAA administrators are selected from among the heads (governors/mayors) of the affiliates. The management of PAA significantly influences the affiliates' policies. Therefore, the selection among the heads is predominant in order to secure the uniformity of the policies among the affiliated bodies.

Figure 3.30 shows the distribution of the methods of appointment.

About 49% used mutual elections and about 33% used the concurrent post method. The concurrent post means that the certain mayor regularly accedes to the administrator of the PAA by common consent among the affiliates. The proportion of the case of concurrent post is higher than the case of PAA assembly members' election. As the direct election of the administrator of the PAA is not required by the constitution and the national law, the concurrent post for the administrator is thought to be allowed and well practiced.

Apportionment of expenses

Apportionment of PAA expenses is defined by the PAA statutes. The general standard is provided by the MIC, as follows.

General Standard:

The PAA meets the expenditure with property revenues, charges and fees. When it has deficits, it makes up the difference with burden charge among the affiliated bodies.
There are several types of rules regarding expenses. The typical ones are as follows.

FULLY FLEXIBLE

This type focuses on the flexibility of social and economic change. It does not use a basis, such as per population. The sample style is as follows.

The administrator decides the next fiscal year's budget charge for each affiliate through the approval of the PAA assembly.

This type secures full flexibility, but every year the affiliates renegotiate the financial burdens. Moreover, from the outside, it is difficult to understand the financial relationships between the PAA and each of its affiliates.

VARIABILITY ORIENTED

This type makes focuses on the variability of the expense burden based on the idea that the apportionment responds if administrative demands on affiliates increase.
The following calculation bases of the apportionments are typical.

(e.g.) per population
per population of the specific region
per number of students
per quantity of water supply.

STABILITY ORIENTED

This type focuses on the stability of the expense burden. If this style were adopted, the amount of the burden would not change. For the affiliates, it is easier to know what to expect to pay to the PAA each year.
The following calculation bases of the apportionment are typical.

(e.g.) per capita
fixed share
per number of houses.

In many cases, several bases are adopted and mixed in a calculated formula that is stated in a PAA statute.

Management of PAA

This section discusses the management of the PAAs in two parts: administrative control and financial control.

Administrative control

"Each local government shall, in performing its affairs, make best efforts to achieve the maximum effects with the minimum expenses for the welfare of the inhabitants" (Article 2(14), LAL). This article is applied to PAAs as special local governments as well as to the ordinary local governments. When a PAA has been organized, it employs staff and manages like a local government. To manage with minimum costs, control of the size of the staff is crucial. Figure 3.31 shows the variation in staff sizes.

There are many small PAAs with 10 or fewer staff members, which is proportionally the dominant staff size. Most PAAs are organized by the affiliates and, in 2012, 1,507 PAAs had affiliates that were all municipalities (97.5%), as is shown in Table 3.3. Figure 3.31 demonstrates that staff size is generally small.

Figure 3.32 shows the total number of employees of PAAs per size of PAA.

The number of PAAs with more than 400 staff, which is the largest PAA, is small. However, considering the total number of employees, the large PAAs have as many as 25,000 staff. Therefore, it is important to consider the large disparities among PAAs in their sizes and that the employment by the large PAAs has a significant effect on the overall employment situation among PAAs.

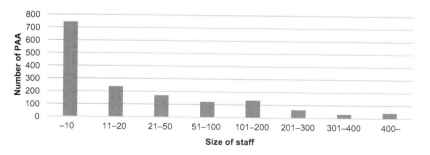

Figure 3.31 Variation in staff size among PAAs, 2012

Source: Created by the author using *"Survey of the system of joint administration in 2014."*

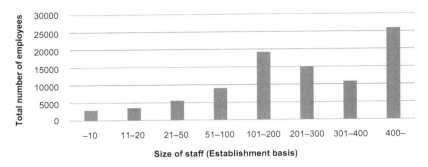

Figure 3.32 Total number of employees per size of establishment basis

Source: Created by the author using "*Survey of the system of joint administration in 2014.*"

Financial control

REVENUE

The revenue structure of PAAs has these features:

1 PAAs have no taxation in in Japan and they have no tax revenue.
2 In 2012, the ratio of national governmental disbursements for PAAs is 4%.

Figure 3.33 shows the sources of revenue of PAA; the ratio of the burden charge by the affiliates is the largest ratio (73%) and the ratio of the national governmental disbursements is relatively small (4%) compared with that of all the local governments (Figure 3.33).

As a practical matter, in the administrative areas of the environmental sanitation and the fire protection, that are the basis of many PAAs, there are small national disbursements.

(Reference) The total revenue for all local governments in national treasury disbursements was 15.5% (Figure 3.34). This shows the fact that the ratio of national disbursements of PAAs is much lower than that of all local governments.

Under these conditions, PAAs are forced to depend on the burden charges of the affiliates. Therefore, PAAs should pay attention to the following points for revenue management.

1 PAAs should closely consult their affiliates, particularly regarding expensive projects, such as replacing public facilities, because their

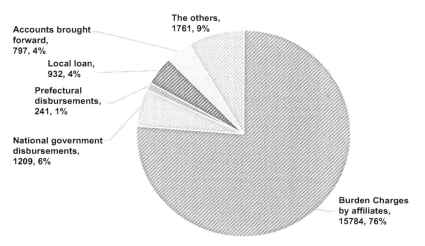

Figure 3.33 Sources of revenue of PAA as of FY 2012 settlement

Source: Created by the author using "*Survey of the system of joint administration in 2014.*"

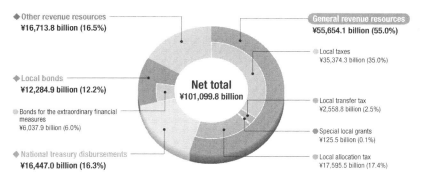

Figure 3.34 Revenue of all local governments (FY 2013 Settlement)

Source: "*White paper on local public finance, 2015 (FY 2013 Settlement),*" MIC.

contributions to the PAA would have a large influence on the affiliates' financial conditions.

2   PAAs should work to secure national disbursements whenever possible.
3   PAAs should work to ensure the receipt of non-tax revenue, such as charges, fees, and disposal of public facilities.

EXPENDITURES

The structure of PAA expenditures has several features.

1 Personnel expenditures dominate expenditures, at 47% (Figure 3.35).

   When all the types of local government are included, personnel expenditures are about 24% (Figure 3.36).
   Thus, the PAA financial structure has markedly high personnel expenses.

2 The goods expenditure (16%) and the ordinary construction expenditure (11%) are the next most expensive types of items.

Based on this breakdown of expenditures, PAAs should pay attention to the following points for expenditure management.

1 Personnel expenditure should be controlled by controlling the staff size, which has a downward rigidity disposition.

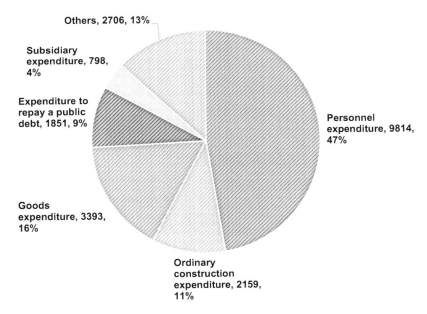

Figure 3.35 Distribution of PAA expenditures by type

Source: Created by the author using *"Survey of the system of joint administration in 2014."*

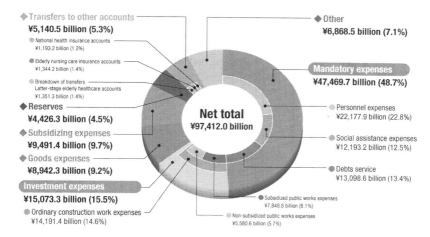

◆Transfers to other accounts
¥5,140.5 billion (5.3%)
　●National health insurance accounts
　　¥1,193.2 billion (1.2%)
　●Elderly nursing care insurance accounts
　　¥1,344.2 billion (1.4%)
　●Breakdown of transfers
　　Latter-stage elderly healthcare accounts
　　¥1,351.3 billion (1.4%)
◆Reserves
¥4,426.3 billion (4.5%)
◆Subsidizing expenses
¥9,491.4 billion (9.7%)
◆Goods expenses
¥8,942.3 billion (9.2%)
Investment expenses
¥15,073.3 billion (15.5%)
　●Ordinary construction work expenses
　　¥14,191.4 billion (14.6%)

◆Other
¥6,868.5 billion (7.1%)

Mandatory expenses
¥47,469.7 billion (48.7%)
　●Personnel expenses
　　¥22,177.9 billion (22.8%)
　●Social assistance expenses
　　¥12,193.2 billion (12.5%)
　●Debts service
　　¥13,098.6 billion (13.4%)
　●Subsidized public works expenses
　　¥7,848.8 billion (8.1%)
　●Non-subsidized public works expenses
　　¥5,580.6 billion (5.7%)

Net total
¥97,412.0 billion

Figure 3.36 Expenditure breakdown among all of the types of local governments by type of expenditure (FY 2013 Settlement)

Source: Created by the author using *"Survey of the system of joint administration in 2014."*

2　PAA is responsible for so many different services and matters that replacement of public facilities should be anticipated. To attain stable financial management of a PAA and the affiliates, the PAA should devise a replacement plan in the early stages of administration and attempt to level its financial burdens.

Issues of PAA

Opinions of the affiliates

PAA has been thought to have both merits and demerits. What do the affiliates think about the current wide-area government? When we consider this subject a survey suggests several points. The results of the survey which was carried out on December 31, 2012, are shown in Table 3.6.

Among the methods, concerning PAA, the ratio of the answer that the issues exist is 32.4% and much higher than the others. Therefore, PAAs have been facing not a few problems to be solved.

Regarding PAA problems, the survey found as follows:

1　Regarding PAA problems, the top most common problems were "It's hard to have urgent decision-making" and "It's hard to reflect affiliate bodies' opinions" (Figure 3.37).

Table 3.6 The issues of wide-area government (as of December 31, 2012)

Method of wide-area administration	Municipalities which operate wide-area administration (Respondent)	Answer: The issues exist (Multiple answers allowed).												Answer: The issues do not exist.	
		Total		Issues of wide-area administration								The others			
				It's hard to have urgent decision making.		It's hard to reflect affiliate bodies' opinions.		Where responsibilities lie is not clarified.		It's hard to get necessary information for business from affiliated bodies.					
		Number of answers	Share (%)	Number of answers	Share (%)	Number of answers	Share (%)	Number of answers	Share (%)	Number of answers	Share (%)	Number of answers	Share (%)	Number of answers	Share (%)
Partial-affairs association	1,623	526	32.4	413	78.5	218	41.4	79	15.0	61	11.6	49	9.3	1,097	67.6
Wide-area union	1,578	412	26.1	271	65.8	176	42.7	102	24.8	41	10.0	43	10.4	1,166	73.9
Council	664	174	26.2	149	85.6	61	35.1	32	18.4	14	8.0	15	8.6	490	73.8
Joint establishment of organs and such	708	109	15.4	74	67.9	28	25.7	21	19.3	14	12.8	16	14.7	599	84.6
Delegation of duties	1,106	145	13.1	69	47.6	56	38.6	22	15.2	27	18.6	24	16.6	961	86.9

Source: Created by the author using "Survey of the system of transactions of municipalities" (December 31, 2012, MIC).

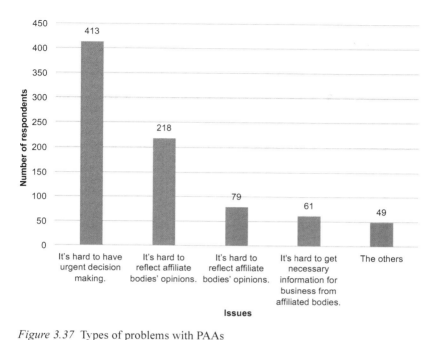

Figure 3.37 Types of problems with PAAs

Source: Created by the author using "*Survey of the system of transactions of municipalities.*"

2   Regarding council matters, 26.2% reported that there are problems, compared to 32.4% who reported that the PAA has problems. Among specific problems, "It's hard to have urgent decision-making" was commonly mentioned (Figure 3.38).

3   Regards of matters of delegation of duties, 13.1% reported that problems exist, which was less than half of the percentage that reported there are problems with PAA. Specifically, "It's hard to have urgent decision-making" was again the most common problem stated. In addition, "It's hard to get necessary information for business from affiliates" was reported by 18.6% of the respondents, which is a remarkably high percentage (Figure 3.39).

Major sources of discontent regarding PAAs concerned "running out of time" and "an imperfect reflection of views of the affiliates." In many PAAs, the head of the chief executives are appointed among the heads of the affiliates, and substantial decision-making is based on consensus among the affiliates.

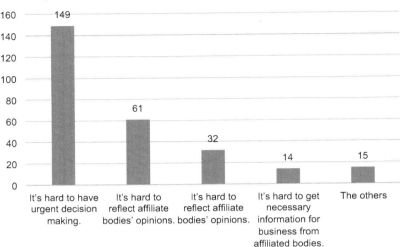

Figure 3.38 Types of problems with the councils

Source: Created by the author using *"Survey of the system of transactions of municipalities."*

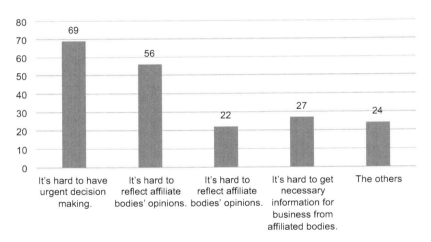

Figure 3.39 Types of problems with the delegation of duties

Source: Created by the author using *"Survey of the system of transactions of municipalities."*

Those structures often seem related to these concerns. Compared to the PAA, the council seems to have fewer problems that take a long time to achieve consensus, but it is easier to include the affiliates in the decisions (Figure 3.38).

Concerning delegation of duties, the insufficiency of necessary information for business seems to be the problem that needs to be addressed, but the amount of discontent was much lower here than regarding the other types of administration (Figure 3.39).

Overall, the affiliates want more rapid decision-making and adequate consideration of their opinions, which leads them to simpler and more flexible administrative approaches.

Simplification of the system

Another problem for the PAAs is the need to simplify the system. The distribution in the number of affiliates is shown in Figure 3.40.

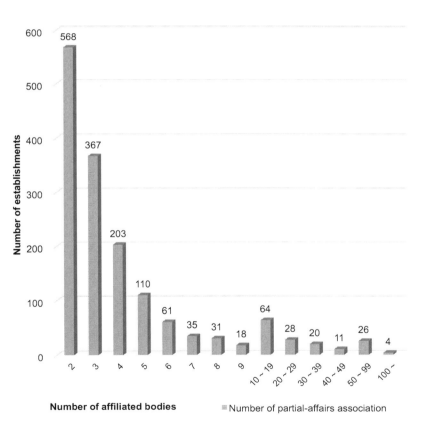

Figure 3.40 Distribution of affiliates as of 2012

Source: Created by the author using "*Survey of the system of joint administration in 2014.*"

Table 3.7 Distribution of the number of affiliates

Number of affiliated bodies	Number of partial-affairs associations	Share	Accumulated Share
2	568 (587)	36.7%	36.7%
3	367 (376)	23.7%	60.5%
4	203 (203)	13.1%	73.6%
5	110 (111)	7.1%	80.7%
6	61 (59)	3.9%	84.7%
7	35 (37)	2.3%	86.9%
8	31 (30)	2.0%	88.9%
9	18 (19)	1.2%	90.1%
10–19	64 (60)	4.1%	94.2%
20–29	28 (30)	1.8%	96.1%
30–39	20 (18)	1.3%	97.3%
40–49	11 (11)	0.7%	98.1%
50–99	26 (27)	1.7%	99.7%
100+	4 (4)	0.3%	100.0%
Total	1546 (1,572)	100.0%	—

Source: Created by the author using "*Survey of the system of joint administration in 2014*" (MIC).

The number varies widely; the largest exceeds 100 and the smallest is two. About 36.7% of all PAAs are those whose number of affiliates is two (mini-PAA) (Table 3.7).

The percentage is not low, but it demonstrates overall inefficiency because the purpose is to join efforts. In some cases, the delegation of duties administrative approach would be more appropriate because the necessity of an independent office and staff might be ambiguous.

The relationship of the number of municipalities and the number of mini-PAAs by prefecture is shown in Figure 3.41 ($r = .35$), demonstrating a weak relationship.

This means that the number of mini-PAAs does not closely relate to the number of municipalities. Currently, mini-PAAs are believed to be because of consecutive municipal consolidations and other historical factors.

When these facts are considered together, the way forward for wide-area administration is to make a "flexible transition" from a PAA to one of the other methods. In some cases of a mini-PAA, it would be most reasonable to

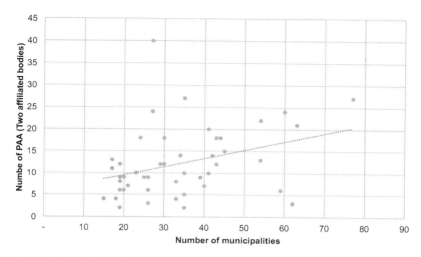

Figure 3.41 Relationship of the number of municipalities and the number of mini-PAAs by prefecture

Source: Created by the author using *"Survey of the system of joint administration in 2014."*

transition to a delegation of duty or to a joint establishment of organ because of the costs of downsizing, as an initial move. After that, when the situation changes, a further transition may be required. Flexibility is required in today's local governments.

Notes

1 In this section, the author relies on the following source: Bas Denters et al., *"Size and Local Democracy,"* EE, which empirically analyses this theme.

2 RAZs were classified as two types. The basic type is the regional municipal zone (RMZ). A RMZ generally required a population of 100,000 or more. It comprises cities and their adjacent farms, mountains, and fishing villages. It should have the capacity to satisfy almost all of the usual demands of citizens. The other type of RAZ was the "large city outer area administrative zone (LOZ)." The details are described in Chapter 4.

3 The purpose of the regional administrator is to devise a plan to promote a RMZ and serve as liaison and coordinator regarding the implementation of that plan. Regarding the fulfillment of responsibilities based on the plan, it was stipulated that the regional administrator was responsible. With that in mind, the PAA was recommended as the type of administrator. When the administrator takes the form of a council, it was stipulated that it should make efforts to abolish itself and establish a PAA.

4 Supreme Court Judgment March 27, 1963/vol. 17, Supreme Courts Reports (criminal cases) 2,121.
5 This is different than the French EPCI and the special districts in the US.
6 This act is approved in accord with the principle of plural intentions in one direction to produce a judicial public effect.

4   Change of the structure

Outline

In this chapter, we examine the changes to the structure of wide-area (regional) government. In December of 2008, before the end of the Great Heisei Consolidation, the MIC issued the "Guidelines for the Promotion of the Concept of Autonomous Settlement Zones." At the same time, the "Guidelines for the Planning of Regional Administration Zones of 2000" were abolished. The autonomous settlement zone (ASZ) was formed as the result of an accumulation of one-to-one agreements concluded on their own initiatives between central cities and their peripheral municipalities.

The following are the three fundamental changes to local governments:

1   In the regional administrative zone (RAZ), the key idea is to raise the level of public services in the whole area. However, in the ASZ, the idea of the spillover of the function from a relevant central city to the neighboring municipalities has been newly adopted.
2   In RAZ, the commonality among the affiliated governments is the basic idea. By organizing a PAA or a council, the affiliated governments establish a comprehensive institution for dealing with the regional administrative agenda. However, in ASZ, the one-to-one contract style is adopted.
3   In RAZ, a systemic transition was popular. The central government promoted the establishment of a council or a partial-affairs association (PAA) for the core governments of the RAZs. A major problem was determining how best to move forward with those new mechanisms. In ASZ, the local governments enter a collaborative agreement without forming any type of organization. The transformation from the

organizational cooperation to the substantial agreement is the observed change of the regional development method. In the analysis of those changes, we examine the outline of the systems.

Wide-area administration zones

History

National promotion of RAZ at the end of the 1960s identified it as a regional administrative policy. The idea was to develop a comprehensive plan to encompass all of the municipalities into an area of interest. Starting in the late 1960s, as vehicular transportation increased, the size of the area within which residents managed their daily lives, including commuting to school, places of employment, commercial centers, and so on, expanded beyond their municipalities. In response, the 12th Local Government System Research Council released a report in 1968 that referred to a need to confirm, as a policy for promoting regional society, a concept which envisages cities destined to become core cities and the farming, mountain, and fishing villages on their periphery as a single unit. The report further pointed out a need to take forward regional administrative systems that have resulted from the pattern whereby local public bodies deal with duties on a joint, shared basis. The Ministry of the Interior (now the Ministry of Internal Affairs and Communications, or MIC) used the report to issue the "Guidelines for Measures to Promote Regional Municipal Zones in Fiscal 1969." This was the beginning of the RAZ policy.

The structure of RAZ

The idea

A detailed policy was unveiled in the report of the 13th Local Government System Research Council. The ideas can be summarized in following points.[1]

1   The RAZ area is composed of several municipal areas. The goal was to establish a RAZ as an everyday zone in which citizens could carry out their daily business and expand their business to cover ever wider geographic areas. Furthermore, by means of joint administration of municipal services, the arrangement of facilities and the management of duties regarding RAZs, such as roads, firefighting, ambulance services and medical care, public hygiene and sanitation, education and

culture, social welfare, and the promotion of industry, would be moved forward under the regional comprehensive plans. That would make it possible to reach solutions to many problems faced by municipalities and achieve balanced development across Japan.

2   The notion of actually establishing a regional administrative system covering all municipal zones simply by means of consolidations was difficult to imagine as an actual, real-life solution, and furthermore, it was not appropriate. Therefore, the formula for joint administration of duties was to be used as well as consolidations to create regional administration as a temporary system.

Based on these ideas, RAZ began in 1969. In the RAZ, each newly established wide-area administrative entity would formulate a regional municipal plan. The administrators would aim to establish necessary infrastructure in the zone in a comprehensive and planned way based on the plan.

Types

The RAZs were classified as two types. The first type comprised regional municipal zones (RMZ) as the basic type of RAZ. A RMZ area is composed of several municipal areas and RMZ is generally required a population of 100,000 or more and a size that could form, or potentially form, a zone of everyday living. It was determined that the area should satisfy the following specific conditions.

1   The overall size of the RMZ, comprising cities and their adjacent farms, mountains, and fishing villages, should have the capacity to satisfy almost all of the usual demands of residents in terms of employment, daily necessities, medical care, education, culture, entertainment, and so on.
2   In RMZs, there should be urban areas (central urban districts) that possess numerous urban facilities and functions that are sufficient to meet residents' usual demands regarding their daily lives.
3   Transportation and communication facilities and networks should be fully equipped to link the central urban districts to other urban districts as well as to rural settlements inside the RMZ.

The other type of RAZ was LOZ (the large city outer administrative zone), which was added to RAZ in 1977. LOZ was specifically about the development of the areas on the periphery of large cities. These areas were not initially covered by RAZ. The purpose of a LOZ was to promote regional government comparable to that of RMZ. The specific organizational criteria of LOZ were stipulated as follows.

1   LOZs had populations of about 400,000 people.
2   LOZs had geographic, historic, and cultural characteristics that enabled them to be identified as single units.
3   LOZs had the necessary urban characteristics that enabled unified future visions to be developed and realized.
4   One or another of the municipalities of the WMZ must be excluded.

The administrator of a LOZ was designated as the council, as specified in Article 252-2 of the Local Autonomy Law (LAL). For LOZs, the relatively simple and convenient council was decided upon as the preferred type of administration.

Organization of a RAZ

The governor (of the relevant prefecture) implemented the organization of a RAZ after consulting with the affiliated governments and the minister of the interior. It was assumed in principle that every municipality belonged to a RAZ. It was stipulated that a regional government would develop a wide-area municipal zone plan to forward the zone based on consultation with the prefectural government in which it was located. That plan included (1) fundamental ideas, (2) fundamental plans, and (3) implementation plans.

1   Fundamental ideas were the broad outlines of the future vision of the promotion and development of the geographic area of the RMZ and the policies and mechanisms needed to realize that vision.
2   Fundamental plans had the following two aspects as determined by the fundamental ideas:

   a   The layout of the urban areas and villages, the system of transportation and communication networks, the details of the resources necessary to administer the plan over a wide area, and the methods of managing the resources.
   b   The resources necessary to the infrastructure with respect to facilities and equipment necessary to implement the actual items.

3   Implementation plans were the specific, concrete details of the requirements for implementing the items referred to in the fundamental plans.

Organization

It was specified that the local governments within a RAZ would, as administrators, form a PAA in accord with Article 284 of the LAL or form a council as specified in Article 252-2-2 of the LAL, to forward the infrastructure and promotion of the RAZ.

The functions of the PAA or the council were to develop a plan to promote the RAZ and serve as liaison and coordinator regarding the plan. Considering those functions, when the relevant local governments formed a council, they should make efforts to abolish the council and establish a PAA as the regional administrator.

The proportional distribution of the types of RAZ administrators in 2008 is shown in Figure 4.1.

There were 86 councils (31%), 158 PAAs (58%), and 31 wide-area unions (11%), suggesting that PAAs played the primary part as RAZ administrators. However, the total number of RAZs decreased after 2003. The explanation of this trend is the Great Heisei Consolidation (1999–2010). As the number of municipalities decreased, the number of RAZ administrators decreased. Moreover, during this time, the number of the councils stabilized at about 86. There was no notable shift from the council type to the PAA

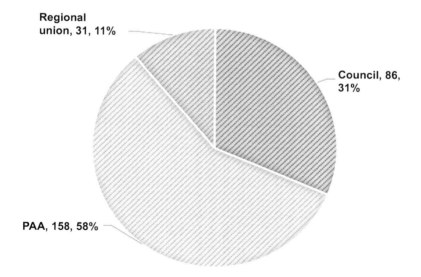

Figure 4.1 Proportional distribution of the types of RAZ administrators (2008)
Source: Created by the author using data from MIC.

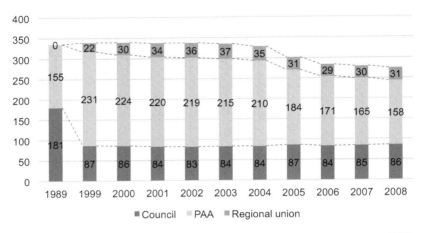

Figure 4.2 Changes to the distribution of the types of RAZ administrators (1989–2008)
Source: Created by the author using data from MIC.

type. Therefore, it is reasonable to conclude that the transition of administrators from council to PAA did not progress as much as the central government had expected (Figure 4.2).

Situation

The number of RAZs and their characteristics in April of 2008 are shown in Table 4.1.

There were 334 RMZs (Regional municipal zones), 25 LOZs (large city outer area administrative zones), and 359 RAZs (Regional administrative zones) altogether. As a percentage of the country overall, the population of the WAZs was 77.6% of the national total, and they constituted 97.1% of the total national land area.

The central government carried out the special financial measures for the support of RAZ: the national grants for the planning cost, the special local bond for the projects of the RAZ, and so forth. However, almost all of Japan was covered by RAZs. So the excessively overbroad setting of RAZs turned down the impact of RAZ as the regional development policy.

The Great Heisei Consolidation (1999–2010) was a major influence on RAZ policy. Two issues emerged. First, the number of affiliated municipalities remarkably decreased as consolidations progressed. Figure 4.3 shows the changes in the numbers of municipalities across Japan and the average numbers of municipalities affiliated with RMZs.

Table 4.1 Characteristics of RAZ, 2008

Categories	Number of zones	Number of affiliates	Percentages of the total number of municipalities (%)	Average number for one zone	Population (thousand)	Percentages of the total number of municipalities (%)	Area (km²)	Percentages of the total number of municipalities (%)
RAZ (Regional administration zone)	359	1,702	95.1	4.7	92,604	77.6	361,161	97.1
RMZ (Regional municipal zone)	334	1,503	84.0	4.5	69,114	57.9	350,471	94.2
LOZ (Large city outer area administration zone)	25	199	11.1	8.0	23,490	19.7	10,690	2.9
Total number of municipalities	–	1,788	–	–	119,278	100.0	371,937	100.0

Source: Created by the author using data from MIC.

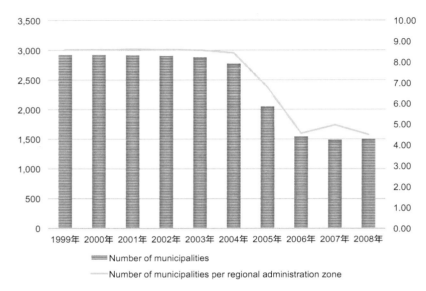

Figure 4.3 Changes in the number of municipalities per RMZ during the Great Heisei Consolidation (1999–2008)

Source: Created by the author using data from MIC.

The total numbers of municipalities affiliated with RMZs were 2,924 in 1999 and 1,503 in 2008. Regarding the decrease in affiliates, the average number of the affiliated municipalities decreased from 8.6 in 1999 to 4.7 in 2010 (Figure 4.3).

Table 4.2 shows the changes in the distribution of the sizes of the municipalities affiliated with RAZs.

However, the number of RAZs comprising three or fewer affiliates increased (Figure 4.4) and the average number of affiliated municipalities in that group decreased from 2.7 to 2.2.

From this, we can conclude that those RAZ affiliates were sub-equal to the RAZs operated by two affiliated municipalities. Those cases present a problem regarding the necessity for a RAZ: is a RAZ requisite for two local governments? The relevant municipalities should consider whether the alternative method of cooperation, such as the delegation of affairs, might be more suitable.[2]

The Great Heisei Consolidation led to what is referred to as a wide-area municipality, meaning that all of a RAZ's affiliated municipalities were merged into a single municipality. In 2008, 37 wide-area municipalities

Table 4.2 Changes to RAZs during the Great Heisei Consolidation, 1999–2008

		Number of RAZ		Number of affiliates (total)		Number of affiliates (average)		Population (average:person)		Area (average:km²)	
		1999	2008	1999	2008	1999	2008	1999	2008	1999	2008
Number of affiliates	1–3	16	157	43	338	2.7	2.2	173,124	162,535	477.60	708.79
	4–6	106	120	545	581	5.1	4.8	182,494	281,829	640.75	907.41
	7–9	113	53	881	382	7.8	7.2	205,851	390,044	895.85	1617.91
	More than 10	129	29	1674	401	13.0	13.8	368,753	631,460	1443.67	1921.27
Total		364	359	3143	1702	8.6	4.7	255,343	258,031	997.32	1007.34

Source: Created by the author using data from MIC.

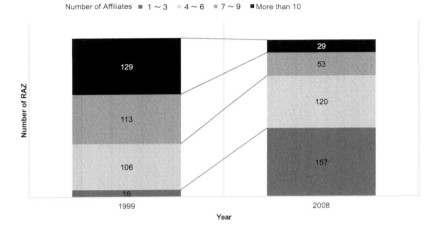

Figure 4.4 Sizes of the numbers of municipalities affiliated with RAZ, 1999 and 2008
Source: Created by the author using data from MIC.

totaling 2,950,000 citizens were produced by the Great Heisei Consolidation. In these cases, there was no purpose to assigning RAZ administrators, and RAZ administrators were abolished in all wide-area municipalities. This phenomenon demonstrates that the RAZ and the Great Heisei Consolidation were somewhat related. Therefore, the RAZ was terminated in 2008 and a new idea for wide-area administration, the ASZ, was developed.

Change to the system

The achievements of the RMZ policies were the road networks that were built across regions and the regional public services, such as waste disposal and fire control, which were developed. However, regional administrations faced three major obstacles.

First, RAZ was limited regarding competencies. Concerning project implementation based on regional municipal plans, the primary implementing administrators were municipalities or prefectures; only a few were PAAs. PAAs were weak regional administrators with respect to exercising force in planning and project development. That is because PAAs had elements of the patched-together municipalities, and it was difficult to plan and implement the massive public investments of a PAA project through those affiliated municipalities. This condition led to constraints on the administrative competency of PAAs.

Second, the Great Heisei Consolidation had a fundamental effect on regional governments. There were 3,229 municipalities in 1999 that decreased to 1,727 in 2010 (see Table 3.1). The average size of the population per municipality was 39,234 in 1999, which grew to 74,150 by 2010. This means that the average size of the basic local governments remarkably changed. There was the additional need to prepare a new structure of municipal cooperation that could accommodate these changes.

Third, Japan's national population began to decline in 2010. The population of Japan was 127 million in 2005, but it is projected to decline to 110 million, a 13% decrease, by 2035. The population of the three major metropolitan areas[3] is projected to decrease by five million, and the other areas are projected to decrease by 11 million in the next 30 years. Urban as well as rural areas are expected to decline; this phenomenon is called the age of depopulation without overcrowded areas, and it is a common modern characteristic of Japanese society. A new idea appropriate to these changes was needed in the post–great consolidation age of the early 21st century.

The autonomous settlement zones

Start of the ASZ

MIC abolished the "Guidelines for the Planning of Wide-area Administration Zones" on March 31, 2000. It then established the new "Guidelines for the Promotion of the Concept of Autonomous Settlement Zones," which was a new policy of regional administration. This was significant because it marked the central government's abandonment of RAZ, which had been in place for 40 years. Thus, there was a major change in regional administration policy with the advent of ASZ as the new approach to regional administration.

ASZ was a way to stem the migration of people from rural areas and reverse that flow of people back into the local jurisdictions. ASZ was formed as the result of an accumulation of one-to-one agreements that concluded on their own initiative between central cities and their surrounding municipalities.

In ASZ, "Selection and Concentration" is a key term that means that it is not reasonable to expect all of the municipalities to provide the full complement of public services, and the national policy should approve regional central cities to provide spillover services. In other words, the citizens of neighboring jurisdictions should be able to use some of the central city's services as regional services, such as medical care, education, shopping, and so on.

The central city of a region should concentrate the urban functions, and the peripheral municipalities should focus on providing daily necessities, such as agricultural production and the conservation of the natural environment.

Intensive functions and network is another key term of ASZ. The cooperation between the central cities and their peripheral municipalities aims to energize the entire region. Through the projects, investments from the private sector are expected to be promoted, the regional economies are expected to be stimulated, and a stable and decentralized society is expected to be produced.

Structure of ASZ

The central city is a city that has already achieved a high level of development regarding such things as large-scale commerce, entertainment, medical care, and daily necessities for the residents. These are private sector as well as administrative functions. The central city needs to be a city that functions not only on behalf of its own residents, but can support peripheral communities as well. Those supports are referred to as "spillover functions." The enrichment of the central city improves the lifestyles of the entire zone and enhances its appeal. In an ASZ, the role of the central city is significant. Its population must be at least 40,000 and, as the center of the zone, the ratio of daytime to nighttime population should be one or higher.

On the other hand, the peripheral municipalities are expected to play a significant part with respect to the environment, community, food production, history, and culture.

The idea of an ASZ is to secure all of the necessities of an entire region through effective agreements between the central city and the peripheral municipalities and by creating an attractive zone.

Characteristics of an ASZ

In 2008, the Local Government System Research Council presented the idea of an autonomous settlement region. The idea is that neighboring local municipalities should work together through agreements based on the recognition that there are functional disparities among them. The local municipalities support each other by making use of spillover functions of their principal cities.

The key point is the use of the central city's spillover abilities in medical, transportation, education, industry, and so on. Through agreements, the central city would provide some essential services, such as hospitals, buses, and schools, to the peripheral municipalities according to a basic plan and by individual agreement.

Typically, a central city and a peripheral municipality would mutually agree regarding a necessary public service and the central city would enter agreements with several peripheral municipalities.

The characteristics of an ASZ are as follows.

1   The historical approach to regional public service cooperation is the wide-area administrative methods among constituent local governments. That is, several local governments agree at the same time through either the cooperative association or the public conference. But, the one-to-one agreement is an approach in which two governments mutually agree regarding things such as doctors' holiday pay, subsidies for demand taxis, or costs of community buses. This approach has the merit of individuality and the agreements depend on individual situations.

2   In many cases, central cities and their peripheral municipalities enter cooperative public contracts. For example, the residents of the peripheral municipalities come to the city hospitals, shop at the city center, and send their children to city high schools.

As the populations in the region continue to decrease, this tendency has grown. Those trends are part of the spillover function of the central cities.

As of October in 2015, 95 cities have concluded autonomous settlement zone agreements.

The process of developing an ASZ system

The process of developing an ASZ begins with a "central city declaration" that sets forth the central city's intention to assume a central role in terms of guaranteeing the livelihood functions necessary for the zone as a whole.

Next, the central city enters "agreements to form an ASZ," which are the specific one-to-one agreements that they enter with the peripheral governments. These agreements aim to safeguard the livelihood functions that ensure the residential population's stability. A sample of the items in these agreements is shown in Figure 4.5.

The next step is to decide on a vision for coexistence within the ASZ that incorporates the actual activities to be performed based on the agreement to

---

<Items in the agreement>
- The strengthening of everyday life functions such as medical care, welfare and education,
- The strengthening of transportation, IT infrastructure networks,
- The strengthening of management ability in the zone in terms of such areas as human resource training, staff exchanges, and so on.

Figure 4.5 Items in ASZ agreement

Source: Created by the author using data from MIC.

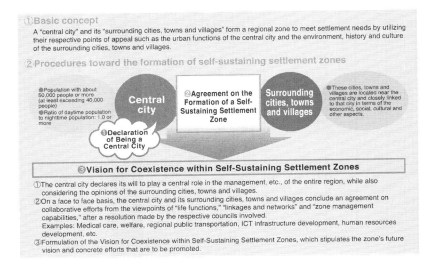

①Basic concept
A "central city" and its "surrounding cities, towns and villages" form a regional zone to meet settlement needs by utilizing their respective points of appeal such as the urban functions of the central city and the environment, history and culture of the surrounding cities, towns and villages.

②Procedures toward the formation of self-sustaining settlement zones

●Population with about 50,000 people or more (at least exceeding 40,000 people)
●Ratio of daytime population to nighttime population: 1.0 or more

Central city

②Agreement on the Formation of a Self-Sustaining Settlement Zone

Surrounding cities, towns and villages

●These cities, towns and villages are located near the central city and closely linked to that city in terms of the economic, social, cultural and other aspects.

①Declaration of Being a Central City

③Vision for Coexistence within Self-Sustaining Settlement Zones

①The central city declares its will to play a central role in the management, etc., of the entire region, while also considering the opinions of the surrounding cities, towns and villages.
②On a face to face basis, the central city and its surrounding cities, towns and villages conclude an agreement on collaborative efforts from the viewpoints of "life functions," "linkages and networks" and "zone management capabilities," after a resolution made by the respective councils involved.
Examples: Medical care, welfare, regional public transportation, ICT infrastructure development, human resources development, etc.
③Formulation of the Vision for Coexistence within Self-Sustaining Settlement Zones, which stipulates the zone's future vision and concrete efforts that are to be promoted.

Figure 4.6 Basic terms and procedures of ASZ

Source: Data from MIC.

form the ASZ and the vision for the future of the zone. It rests on the foundation of separate, individual consultation between the central city and the peripheral governments. The duration of the vision is about five years. The basic ideas and the procedures are shown in Figure 4.6.

The situation of ASZ

As of October of 2015, 128 cities had issued central city declarations; of these, 95 cities had concluded autonomous settlement zone agreements with their peripheral municipalities. Altogether, 92 zones had drawn up visions for coexistence.

ASZ began in 2009 and the number of ASZ agreements has markedly increased since then (Figure 4.7).

This trend shows that many local governments are interested in this new type of inter-municipal cooperation. In the years ahead, the number of zones is expected to continue increasing.

Figure 4.8 shows the correlation between the number of municipalities by prefecture and the number of cities that drew up central city declarations.

The data show that the number of ASZ projects by prefecture is positively related to the number of municipalities ($r = .68$).

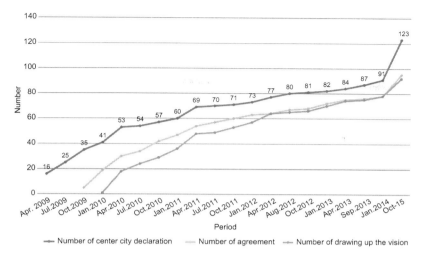

Figure 4.7 Increase in ASZ agreements

Source: Created by the author using data from MIC.

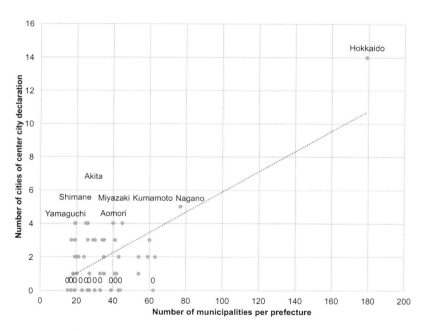

Figure 4.8 The relationship between the number of municipalities by prefecture and number of cities that drew up a central city declaration

Source: Created by the author using data from MIC.

Moreover, the number of ASZ projects is higher in the prefectures whose ratios of decrease are low, as shown in Figure 3.11 (such as Hokkaido, Nagano, Aomori, and Miyazaki).

This finding suggests a reflecting effect. The prefectures and the relevant municipalities that did not consolidate for any regional reasons are still interested in inter-municipal cooperation. These data suggest that the local governments have been pursuing reasonable cooperative frameworks (see Chapter 3).

Operation of ASZ

Figure 4.9 shows the situation of the administrative services adopted by agreements among the ASZ affiliates.

The three most common services are medical care, transportation, and industrial development, and they tend to be in high demand when ASZ structures are establishing spillover functions in a zone.

Medical care

Among the ASZ projects, medical care cooperation is dominant. An image of the ASZ structure of medical care services' provision is shown in Figure 4.10.

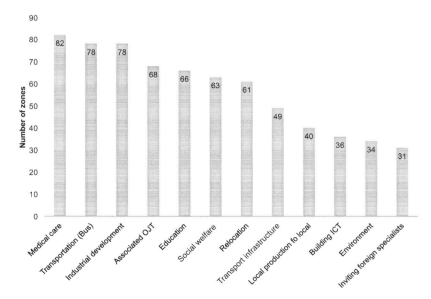

Figure 4.9 Administrative services adopted by ASZ agreements as of October 1, 2014

Source: Created by the author using data from MIC.

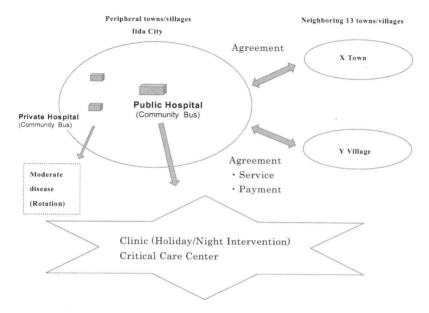

Figure 4.10 Schematic of the ASZ provision of medical care (Iida city case)
Source: Created by the author.

A typical example of an ASZ project is Iida city. Iida city is located in Nagano prefecture. It had a population of about 105,000 in 2010 and an area of 659 km² (Figure 4.11).

In March of 2009, Iida city issued a central city declaration and entered a one-to-one agreement with 12 peripheral municipalities.

One of the main services in those agreements concerned medical care cooperation. Iida city's public hospital has a critical care center and a holiday and overnight emergency care clinic. As a matter of fact, a lot of citizens of the peripheral municipalities came to the care center and the care clinic in Iida city because enough medical services are not provided in those peripheral municipalities. In view of the city function this phenomenon is called the spillover of Iida city's medical care function to the peripheral municipalities.

Thinking of these real situations, Iida city and the peripheral municipalities reached an agreement. The clinic is supported by the doctors of Iida city. The citizens of Iida city can mainly make use the care center and the care clinic. The citizens of the twelve peripheral municipalities can also use the clinic. Iida city and the twelve governments share the costs of the clinic's

Figure 4.11 Location of Iida city in Nagano prefecture
Source: Created by the author using Google Maps.

medical staff. Moreover, an obstetrical surgery clinic and a disaster medical care center are similarly shared.

In this way Iida city hospital is providing a substantial spillover function in the ASZ zone. This hospital is a medical base that has played a principal role in this region and through the ASZ structure these concerned local bodies can establish a legal and stable structure of medical care.

Transportation

Cooperative transportation is the second most important service in ASZ agreements. In many regional zones, the principal urban functions of medical care (e.g., hospital), education (e.g., high school), and consumption (e.g., shopping malls) are concentrated in the central city. Citizens in the peripheral municipalities strongly want access to the central city for these services. Therefore, public transportation (e.g., bus) should be part of the cooperative agreements. A schematic of the transportation services aspect of the ASZ structure is shown in Figure 4.12.

Another typical example of an ASZ project is Hachinohe city. Hachinohe city is located in Aomori prefecture. In 2010 it had a population of 238,000 and an area of 305 km².

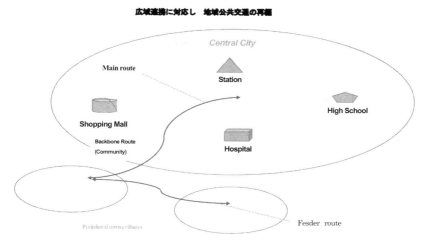

Figure 4.12 ASZ transportation structure
Source: Created by the author.

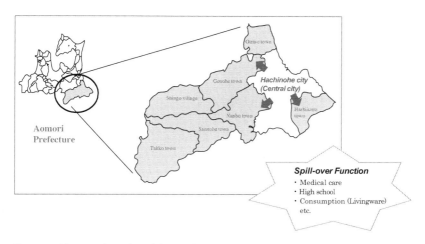

Figure 4.13 Location of Hachinohe city
Source: Created by the author.

In March of 2009, Hachinohe city issued a central city declaration, and it made one-to-one agreements with seven peripheral municipalities (Figure 4.13).

One of the major services in those agreements concerns transportation cooperation. More than 20% of the commuters in four peripheral municipalities travel to Hachinohe city. More than 30% of the inpatients in seven peripheral municipalities use the hospitals in Hachinohe city. For six of the peripheral municipalities, the commodity purchase rates in Hachinohe city exceed 50%.

Based on those close relationships and the spillover functions of Hachihohe city, cooperative agreements for public transportation were made. The central city and each peripheral municipality entered an agreement to plan and implement the zone's public transportation. In that plan, they set the main route and the feeder routes of the bus system. The main route links the urban core points, such as the station, the high school, and the shopping mall, to the peripheral municipalities.

Based on the plan, Hachinohe city and peripheral municipalities maintain the bus routes, and moreover they introduced the cut-rate fare policies for the lines joining the significant points such as hospitals and schools. They also carried out the reduction of waiting times for the connections between the main route and the feeder routes.

The significance of ASZ

These trends of ASZ result in a new style of regional development. In this structure, two changes are remarkable:

1   The way of cooperation changed, shifting from the way of setting an organization to the way of formulating the substantial agreements. Under the policy of setting up the RAZ establishing the organizations as administrators are made much of. However recently the policy of ASZ the contents of one-to-one agreement is thought to be crucial. That the interested local governments can focus on the contents of agreement through negotiating with each other is one of the substantial merit in view of policy making for the regional development.
2   The agreement style changed, shifting from the joint agreement to one-to-one agreement. The RAZ policy was mainly based on PAA as its regional administrator. PAA is established based on the joint legal act by several local governments. This act is approved in accord with the principle of plural intentions in one direction to produce a judicial public effect. On the other hand, the recent style ASZ is based on the contract between one central city to the other neighbor municipality. This new style brings some effects. First, it leads the more flexible inter-municipal relationship. Responding to the social change between two local governments, they can change the contents of the agreement more easily and more swiftly than the case of the joint legal act among several local governments. Second the responsibility of the interested government is clearer in a one-to-one agreement.

Japanese society has entered an era of depopulation as a society, and the rural areas are experiencing a more remarkable decline than the urban areas. Therefore, the core urban services, such as hospitals, schools, and shopping malls, have become more scattered and less accessible to rural residents. It also is becoming more important to find ways to link those services to the people who need them. At present, medical and transportation services are the most popular aspects of ASZ agreements in many regions.

Under those situations the flexible and substantial inter-municipal cooperation will become more and more significant. Therefore ASZ style can be expected for the contemporary community renovation.

Notes

1 Report of the 12th Local Government System Research Council (August 27, 1968).
2 Among the 59 RAZs that constituted two affiliated bodies, 14 RAZs were abolished.
3 Three metropolitan areas are Tokyo Metropolitan area, Kinki area (which includes Osaka city), and Chuukyo area (in which Nagoya city is located).

5   Conclusion

Consolidation and cooperation

Consolidation

This book examines the structure of wide-area governmental administration in Japan. From the perspective of responding to broad regional needs, local governments have two options: consolidation or cooperation, as shown in Figure 3.3.

A local government's choice of consolidation depends on social factors, such as administrative skills, financial stability, political diversity, social trust, neighborhood integration, local attachment, and association membership. If the relevant authorities, such as the chief executives of a local government, and the citizens prefer the positive social elements of consolidation, they most likely would choose it, that is, amalgamation among jurisdictions. If they do not adopt a consolidation approach, then they would most likely seek cooperation, that is, through a partial-affairs association (PAA) or other type of cooperative association.

Japan has made impressive progress regarding consolidation; since the end of the nineteenth century, the number of municipalities decreased from 71,314 in 1888 to 1,718 in 2014, as shown in Table 3.1.

The question is: why has consolidation dominated? Five factual background reasons help to answer this question.

1   The transition from the traditional village to the administrative village was specifically implemented in 1889 by the Great Meiji Consolidation (Figure 2.1).
2   The timing of the three major amalgamation movements harmonized with social modernization. The 1888 Great Meiji Consolidation occurred just before *Shisei-Chosonsei*, the Municipal Government

Act that aimed to establish the first local administrative legal system (implemented in 1888). Modernization was a salient social topic, and the relevant authorities wanted to improve local governments' basic competencies. Then, the Great Showa Consolidation occurred between 1953 and 1956. At that time, Japan's economy was in the beginning of a high-growth period. The demand to enlarge public services was strong. In that context, municipalities' appropriate operation of junior high schools was a focal agenda item, and the Great Showa consolidation was conducted to establish that school system. The Great Heisei Consolidation occurred between 1999 and 2010. Several factors were important, but, perhaps the most important factor was decentralization. When the Comprehensive Decentralization Act was devised at the end of the twentieth century, strengthening the local governments' systems was considered requisite. Thus, the societal context that emerged from social modernization pushed the consolidation of local governments.

3   The consolidation of Japan's local governments was closely related to decentralization. Decentralization has been the most fundamental agenda of Japan's local governments. Numerous reports were written and legislative proceedings were conducted as decentralization progressed. The Comprehensive Decentralization Act (enacted in 1999) made important progress by transferring the legal authorities from the central government to the local governments, and the improvement of local governments' competencies was indispensable. The idea of a fusion of decentralization with consolidation grew into a consensus among the relevant local governments. The Comprehensive Decentralization Act was a driving force in this process.

4   The modern local administrative system (since the end of the nineteenth century) instituted the two-tier system in place of the feudal system that had been present since the Han Dynasty in the village communities in Japan. In the two-tier system, many prefectures took a substantial amount of initiative to promote consolidations, and all of the prefectures drafted consolidation plans; some of them increasingly advised the municipalities under their jurisdictions to consolidate. Although consolidations were not mandatory, they were somewhat under the control of the prefectures.

5   Decentralization has continued to advance, but centralized elements still exist. A major consolidation is not mandatory; however, through the advice and support of the central government, based on the Municipal Merger Special Act, the municipalities were gently and practically pushed toward consolidation.

Cooperation

The cooperation system also has progressed since the end of the nineteenth century. After World War II, Japan's local governments have been adopting several types of wide-area administrative methods stipulated by the Local Autonomy Law (LAL) (Table 3.2), and, as of July 1, 2012, there were 7,921 establishments. Among these systems, the dominant type is the obligation of duties (72%), followed by PAAs (20%) (Figure 3.15). The cooperative systems in the PAA with corporate legal status, their own staffs and budgets, have progressed and filled significant roles in the local governments. Thus, consolidation and cooperation have evolved in Japan.

Concerning the management of wide-area administrations, one option is to maintain the current structure and strategy. If the affiliated local governments agree to preserve the current system, it will continue. However, in that event, wide-area services' organizations, such as PAAs, will be expected to pursue improved administrative skills with respect to effectiveness and development. PAAs are expected to be responsible for financial management and skillful management.

Financial management

PAAs address operational issues. In the revenue structure, PAAs are not provided with external funding, such as national subsidies, as shown in Figure 3.20. Therefore, PAAs are highly dependent upon the affiliated local governments for financing. This financing structure undermines the autonomy of PAAs. The dominant weak point of PAAs from the perspective of their management is difficulty in achieving speedy decision making, as shown in Table 3.6.

Regarding expenditures, the share of personnel to overall expenditures is 47%, as shown in Figure 3.35. All of the local governments spend about 23% on personnel, as shown in Figure 3.36; therefore, in the PAA financial structure, personnel expenditures are remarkably high.

Considering this, PAAs should rigidly control the sizes of staff to limit personnel expenditures. Moreover, regarding preparations to replace public facilities, PAAs should devise the replacement plans in the early stages and aim to equalize the financial burdens of the affiliated governments. From this perspective, consensus about the size of staff and investments is key to expenditure management.

Skillful management

PAAs are given the particular status of quasi-local governmental entities and they are expected to perform advanced administrative tasks similar to ordinary local governments. Therefore, PAA administrators are expected to be leaders of progress in the following three activities:

1   Adopting detailed accounting rules, including balance sheets, to achieve full financial analyses;
2   Creating fixed asset registers of the associations and practice public facility management;
3   Enacting public information release bylaws and comply with requests of public information.

Change to wide-area administration

Background

Consolidation and cooperation have progressed to the present. However, notable changes have been occurring. Two significant social changes are depopulation and fewer local governments.

First, sharp depopulation began in about 2010 when Japan reached a turning point. The population of 128 million in 2010 is projected to decrease to 116 million by 2030 and to 99 million by 2048. This phenomenon relates the other social issues, such as shrinking cities, low birth rates, longevity, a shrinking taxpayer base, and widening regional diversity.

Second, the number of local governments has remarkably decreased. In 1999, the number of municipalities was 3,229, which had decreased to 1,727 in 2010. The average size of the population per municipality increased from 39,234 in 1999 to 74,150 in 2010. The RAZ system was incompatible with those changes, which led to the new structure, the post–Heisei amalgamation structure, as a necessity. In the context of these social changes, the present wide-area administrations have commenced several dramatic changes to their systems.

Proactive transitions

The first option is to undertake a proactive transition of the wide-area services' system to make it more suitable. Some local governments are not satisfied with the current operation of their existing cooperative associations because they take a long time to make decisions.

Currently, the chief executives and assemblies of the associations are the associations' decision makers; however, practically, consensus among the constituent local governments is required. The financial dependency of associations, such as PAAs, is strengthening those structures.

Consequently, it is difficult to obtain a speedy consensus among the individual local governments. The heads of the local governments keenly feel this weakness, particularly regarding PAAs (Table 3.6). Notably, there are some recent cases of the transition from a PAA to the delegation of duties. In 2009, in response to these problems, the 29th Local Government System Research Council issued a report in which it proposed the proactive transition of wide-area services' methods. A rapid transition to a more suitable method of cooperation is anticipated in the field of local administration. Moreover, based on the report, the central government amended the LAL to promote the proactive transition of the wide-area systems to more suitable types. The three following concrete examples of possible scenarios can provide detailed understanding:

1   If the constituent governments preferred quicker decision making by the cooperative association, then a transition to the delegation of duties approach is an option for them because it is generally believed to be a simpler system. Accordingly, the amendment to the law (LAL) in 2012 included a simple process by which an affiliated government could secede from an association (PAA or council). If an affiliated government preferred the council, it could secede simply by means of a legal notice without obtaining the consent of the other governments. Recently, the number of delegation of duties increased from 5,036 in 2006 in 5,688 in 2012 (Figure 3.16).

2   PAAs usually employ staff with organized hierarchies. Sometimes, the labor costs are a heavy burden for the associated governments. In that event, they can transition into the shared administrative organization, which means that several governments share a certain administrative position. This type of system would improve the efficiency of an organization and is acceptable.

3   If a PAA fundamentally changes, the other options might be more suitable than the PAA. For example, if a PAA stops operating public facilities and focuses instead on a software business venture, a change from that PAA to a council would be appropriate because said change would not require assets or exclusive staff (see the merits of PAA, Table 3.4).

In these three scenarios, proactive change is essential and expected and would lead to the diversification of methods for wide-area public services. Moreover, one-to-one agreement in the ASZ structure is expected to be the more flexible approach. In other words, local governments can easily amend their agreements to be in accord with changes at the regional level. In this way, proactive transition is a key for current wide-area administrations (Figure 5.1).

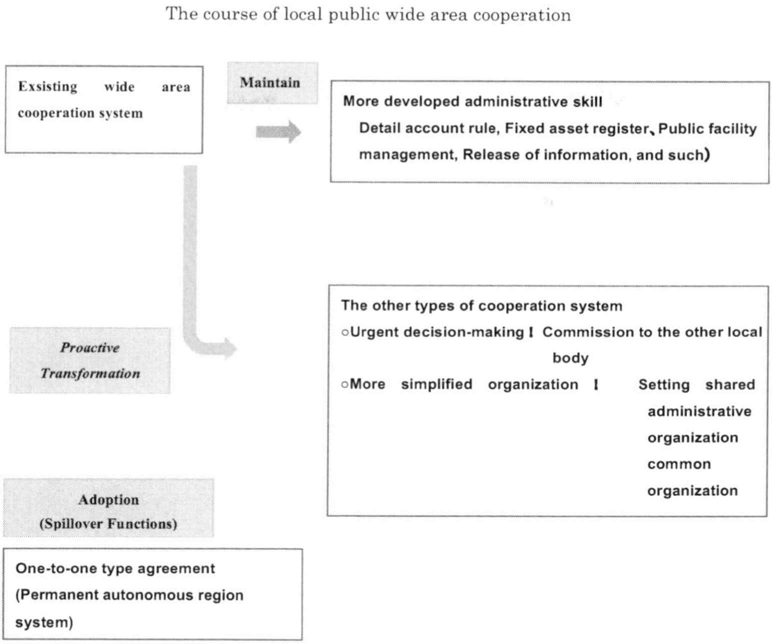

The course of local public wide area cooperation

| Exsisting wide area cooperation system | **Maintain** ⇒ | More developed administrative skill

Detail account rule, Fixed asset register, Public facility management, Release of information, and such) |

| *Proactive Transformation* | | The other types of cooperation system
○Urgent decision-making ❙ Commission to the other local body
○More simplified organization ❙ Setting shared administrative organization common organization |

Adoption (Spillover Functions)

One-to-one type agreement (Permanent autonomous region system)

Figure 5.1 The process of governmental cooperation

Source: Created by the author.

Departure from the uniformity

Background

The traditional basic idea of Japanese local government has been to establish the norm of the national minimum and the standard of raising up the whole regional service by which the citizens are provided the same levels of public services across regions.

This idea has been primary in Japan since its postwar rehabilitation efforts of the 1950s. The central government and the local governments set the goals regarding infrastructure and public facilities, such as roads and clean, ample water supplies.

These goals were set higher than the national minimum so that the governments would be able to guarantee the minimum standards for necessities closely related to the lives of citizens. RAZ was the typical policy for improving the standards of public services, using the unitary mechanism. RAZ regards cities that are destined to become core cities with farming, mountain, and fishing villages on their peripheries as single units. In other words, the idea was to develop a total region so that all of the citizens within an area could enjoy urban public services. By organizing a PAA or council, the affiliated local governments established comprehensive institutions to manage the wide-area administrative agenda according to this vision.

Between the 1940s and the 2000s, the several actors became interrelated and complementary: the central government pursued local administrative modernization, the industrial circles sought high growth, and the citizens demonstrated a need for improved public services. However, limits emerged at the beginning of the twenty-first century.

Approving the spillover function

The declining birthrate and a growing proportion of elderly people, the dramatic depopulation, and the tight state finances began in Japan at the beginning of the twenty-first century.

In this context, the ASZ system began as a new regional development policy strategy. First, the idea that all the municipalities should take on the full set of public service functions falls into difficulty. And the idea changed from raising the level of the total unit to approving the spillover functions of the central city in the region: the functions regarding healthcare, transportation, education, industry, and so on.

The idea was that the adjacent local governments should rely on each other by recognizing that functional disparities exist among them and they should support each other by using the spillover function of their central cities.

The ASZ scheme is based on the idea of the spillover function of the central city toward the peripheral governments, and it aims to support and enhance those cooperative relationships. Through agreements, the principal (city) government provides some essential services, such as hospitals, buses, and schools, to the peripheral governments under a general plan and individual agreements.

Typically, a central city and a peripheral municipal government agree on required public services, and the city enters these agreements with several peripheral governments. In this system, the central city in the zone allows its resources, such as healthcare, social welfare supports, and transportation, to spill over to the peripheral governments. The examples are the medical care in the zone of Iida city and peripheral municipalities and the transportation service in the zone of Hachinohe city and the peripheral municipalities.

Under the conditions of an aging society, depopulation, and tight state finances, a change has been seen from the unitary national minimum. The local governments have entered an era of being required to change the policy of public services.

The concentration of the functions and the networking of them in the region is a key policy. In other words, it means a farewell to bottom-up development. The regional policy has reached the stage of diversity based on regionally specific cooperation needs. This is distinct from raising the level of the total unit, but supportive of the area by using each local government's functions, including the spillover function.

One-to-one agreement

The second remarkable change in the method adopted by the ASZ system as a regional policy on development is the one-to-one agreement. This method is considered revolutionary in the following two ways.

1   Transition from "the joint agreement" to the "one-to-one agreement." Historically, the wide-area public services' cooperative is a joint agreement among constituent local governments. That is, several local governments agree regarding, for example, the certificate of intention; the statutes of a PAA are simultaneously submitted to each affiliated government's assembly and, upon approval, they are finalized.

     However, a one-to-one agreement is an approach in which two local governments mutually agree regarding some aspect of services, such as wages for doctors who work on holidays, subsidies for demand taxis, or the costs of community buses. This approach has the merit of being individualized to meet regional specific needs because the contents of the agreements depend on the individual situation and on only two governmental entities.

2   Transition from establishing organizations to substantial cooperation. In the WAZ system, systemic transitions are key. The central government promotes establishing a council or a PAA for the regional administrative zone (RAZ) governments and attempts to cultivate them to be responsible for management of the zones. The local governments are expected to devise the plans and offer comprehensive services based on the plans. A significant aspect is devising the ways in which to proceed with those plans. On the other hand, in the case of autonomous settlement zone (ASZ), the local governments focus on the substantial cooperation derived from the contents of their one-to-one agreements. The central cities are expected to be the driving forces in developing the zones and, under their leadership, in approaches that are more convenient and simpler to implement.

This is the observed change in the regional development methods, which also are philosophical changes for the local governments. In other words, these changes mean "farewell to the bottom-up" of regional development policies, suggesting that the local governments should be separated from the improvements made to the region. However, the local governments should stimulate the region proactively by using their resources.

Thus, we can refer to these recent trends as departure from the uniformity of wide-area (regional) administration.

Effects of the changes

An overview of the new trends, transitions and one-to-one agreements, has been presented. These two trends could bring essential changes to local development policies.

The key ideas in these trends, introduced into local governmental administration, are flexibility and individuality. The traditional approaches to local development policies have been "unified efficiency of local organization" and "comprehensive bottom-up in order to attain the national minimum," which are important in Japanese local government.

Depopulation is expected to continue into the foreseeable future. Japan's population of 128 million in 2010 is projected to decrease to 99 million by 2048. That trend would shrink the cities and disperse communities. In a context of depopulation, core public utilities (composed of public and private facilities) would scatter throughout the regions. Healthcare, educational services, and obtaining necessities are daily growing more difficult. Moving into an aging population will demand developing spillover and building flexible cooperative ties among local governments as indispensable administrative tasks.

Simultaneously, society will likely face downsizing of its basic infrastructure. From a financial perspective, local governments must implement serious reductions of public facilities and infrastructure, making inter-governmental cooperation on the local level an imperative. In that effort, linking and sharing are key terms. Some local governments have begun considering ways to link their variety of the drainage routes and how to share their gymnastic halls with their neighbors. Regarding relatively new demands to cooperate, the flexible ASZ method will be increasingly important.

It is likely that the downsizing of infrastructure will strongly influence local development policies because this trend means transitioning away from uniformity in Japanese local governments. To the present, Japan has had a stable two-tier local governmental structure, with local cooperative associations. However, that downsizing would have both positive and negative consequences for public policies. On the positive side, a transition to an approach that is more effective and efficient and the adoption of one-to-one agreements by local governments would likely bring improve administrative skills and increase diversity. Moreover, diversity and regional individuality could lead to stronger local autonomy.

However, there are disadvantages in that the differences between the central and peripheral governments could, in some cases, impede lessening of power disparities among the local governments' administrations. The systems also will likely become more complex.

In the field of public administration, mobility, mutability, and pragmatism are preferred. The current trend is typical in that context. However, the mobility of the system involves the risks of instability and complexity. Growing out of the uniformity of regional development policies accompanies those risks. Therefore, we should acknowledge that deliberate strategies for future community development are strongly required for Japan.

References

Akio Kamiko, *The Start of Modern Local Government (1868–1880)* [Historical Development of Japanese Local Governance vol. 1, National Graduate Institute for Policy Studies] (2010).

Bas Denters et al., *Size and local democracy* (EE, 2014).

Eiji Tajika and Yuji Yui, *Fiscal Decentralization in Japan: Tackling Japan's Fiscal Challenges* (IMF, 2006).

Hideaki Matsumoto, *Chikujou Chihoujichihou* [Article-by-article Commentary of Local Autonomy Law] (Tokyo, 2009).

Hiroshi Kikagawa, *Chihouseido Shousi* [Brief History of Japanese Local Autonomy] (Keisou Shobou, 1986).

Kiyotaka Yokomichi, *The Development of Municipal Mergers in Japan* [Up-to-date Documents on Local Autonomy in Japan No. 1] (National Graduate Institute for Policy Studies, 2008).

Kiyotaka Yokomichi, *New Policies in Wide-area Administration in Japan* [Up-to-date Documents on Local Autonomy in Japan No. 6] (National Graduate Institute for Policy Studies, 2010).

Kurt Steiner, *Local Government in Japan* Stanford University Press, (CA, 1965).

Osamu Koike, *Local Government and National Development: Evolution of Local Autonomy in Postwar Japan* (EROPA Local government center, 1998).

Michio Muramatsu, *Local Government Development in Post-war Japan* Oxford University Press, (NY, 2001).

Ministry of Internal Affairs and Communications, *Chihoujichi Geppou* [Local Autonomy Monthly Report No. 54 and No. 55] MIC (Tokyo, 1999–2012).

Ministry of Finance Japan, http://www.mof.go.jp/english/index.htm.

Nihon Toshi Center, *Jinkougenshoujidai ni okeru Chiikikoukyoukoutsuu no arikata* (Nihon Toshi Center, 2015).

Nobuki Mochida, *Local Government Organization and Finance: Japan: Local Governance in Industrial Countries* (The World Bank, 2006).

Shigeru Yamashita, *Taikei Hikaku Chihou Jichi* [System Comparison of Local Autonomy] (Gyousei, Tokyo, 2010).

Shunsuke Kimura, *Kouikirenkei no Shikumi* [System of Regional cooperation] (Daiichihoki, Tokyo, 2015).

Shunsuke Kimura, A Multilayered Check-and-Balance System: Trends of a Dual Representative System in Japanese Local Administration, *Hitotsubashi Journal of Law and Politics*, 42 (2014), pp. 25–50.

Shunsuke Kimura, Goals and Reforms of Current Japanese Local Tax System, *Hitotsubashi Journal of Law and Politics*, 43 (2015), pp. 17–48.

Teijuu jirituken kousou kennkyuukai, *Teijuu jiritukenn kousou Handbook* [Autonomous Settlement Zone System Handbook] (Gyousei, Tokyo, 2010).

Toshiyuki Otaki, *America no Chiho Jichi* [Local Government in America] (Daiichihoki, Tokyo, 2004).

Tsutomu Muroi and Shou Harano, *Shin Gendai Chihoujichihou Nyuumon* [ABC of New Modern Local Autonomy Law] (Houritu-Bunkasha Kyoto, 2005).

Index